10^{50}

ENGLISH GARDEN EMBROIDERY

ENGLISH GARDEN EMBROIDERY

Over 80 Original Needlepoint Designs of Flowers, Fruit and Animals

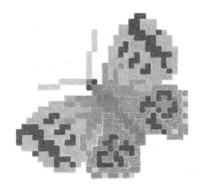

STAFFORD WHITEAKER

BRACKEN BOOKS

LONDON

FOR MY DAUGHTER, VICTORIA

Originally published by Century Editions, an imprint
of the Random Century Group Ltd,
20 Vauxhall Bridge Road,
London SW1V 2SA

This edition published 1992 by Cresset Press and
distributed by Bracken Books, an imprint of Studio
Editions Limited, Princess House, 50 Eastcastle Street,
London W1N 7AP, England

ISBN 1 85170 974 6

Designed by Clare Clements
Artwork by Colin Salmon and Lindsay Blow
Embroidery executed by Stanley Duller

Cover: charted patterns for Little Owl and
Spring Flowers are shown on pp. 69 and 118

Set in Linotron ITC Cheltenham
by SX Composing Ltd, Rayleigh, Essex

Printed and bound in Italy
by New Interlitho S.p.a., Milan

CONTENTS

INTRODUCTION

Embroidery and flower gardening are both decorative arts and for centuries those who love gardens have brought plants and flowers into their embroideries and, equally, those who love to embroider have sought inspiration in the garden and often the pleasure of tending it themselves.

What greater delight is there than to behold the earth apparelled with plants as with a robe of imbroidered worke set with orient pearles and garnished with great diversitie of rare and costly jewels?

The Herbal, John Gerard, 1597

There has been a long history of the use of patterns in embroidery and various forms of the patterns, whether painted on canvas or charted, as in this book, continue to be employed by embroiderers. Charted patterns, usually done on graph paper in black and white squares, each representing a stitch, were popular until after the Second World War. Since then the painted canvas, whether done by hand, which is expensive, or by silk screen process, has been widely sold. Canvas with a painted design dictates the design shape and permits little variation in either the design or the background or the colours. All this puts limitations on the embroiderer's own creative and interpretative talents. In the charted design, colour selection may be recommended but can be discarded and background colours are usually left to the discretion of the embroiderer.

In spite of the recent liberating of needlework from traditional designs and stitches into the realm of 'creative art', the great majority of embroiderers still prefer the long-time favourite motifs and patterns of flowers, fruit and animals.

It seemed to me that there might be many needlepoint workers who would enjoy a collection of new patterns based on the same concept as the coloured and graphed ones so popular in the nineteenth century which were called Berlin Artwork. I suspect, too, that a lot of embroiderers like myself can easily learn how to do needlepoint from the many interesting books available

No English garden would be complete without an apple tree bearing delicious fruit and offering summer shade.

but that a whole selection of patterns is not so readily at hand. Borrowing patterns from others means taking great care of them and, as I often pencil in notes to help with my counting of stitches and make remarks about the work in progress, borrowing patterns is inconvenient. Patterns also need to be kept for later reference in case you want to use a flower or border from one pattern in another needlepoint. I favour simple stitches like cross and tent and don't greatly fancy modern interpretative embroidery which often seems to be all strings, hanging wool and three dimensional abstractions. For me, it has the same harshness and coldness of much of the architecture of the last thirty years.

With comments on the flowers and plants divided up by the seasons of the year, quotations from amusing or thoughtful poems, and notes on the history of embroidery, my aim has been to create a pattern book for the literate needlewoman.

HOW THE BOOK IS ORGANIZED

Extensive information on advanced techniques can readily be found, but, as many needlepoint workers may be unsure of stitch methodology, I have included illustrations of basic stitches which serve to remind both the novice and the advanced worker of methods. For each design there are suggested colourways for yarns, coded for both British Appleton's Crewel Wools and American Paterna Persian Wools.

Believing that a lot of instructions about working each pattern would not be particularly constructive, I decided that the text to accompany the designs should strike an informal note which might prove helpful and interpretative for the embroiderer, and one which could be read separately from the pattern itself. Each page-size pattern is therefore accompanied by comments about its style and possibilities; a small charted pattern which may be used alone or sometimes as a complimentary border; some information about the flower or plant portrayed; and one or more poetic sayings which lend themselves to work as an embroidered sampler. An alphabet is given separately for this purpose.

Embroidery uses many of the same senses as does our response to the garden and I thought that the inclusion of recipes for a few delicious dishes might also add to the pleasures of time, place and season. As to my choice of poems and songs and old sayings, some are mere amusements and others meant, hopefully, to give pause for thought.

TERMINOLOGY

Many people seem confused about the 'right' name for needlepoint. This term is heard more in the United States than in England, where the word 'canvaswork' is still frequently used. 'Tapestry' is a term incorrectly applied to needlepoint for it means a woven work. The term embroidery is a general one, and, in England, the expression 'canvaswork embroidery' is deemed correct when expert embroiderers are talking among themselves. In this book I frequently use 'needlepoint' as this is now the most popular term used on both sides of the Atlantic. I also freely interchange the terms 'embroidery', 'canvaswork' and 'needlepoint'. In any conversation at the local crafts college or among friends, one is apt to hear all three expressions used and exchanged for each other – and everyone seems to understand what is being talked about.

For winter's rains and ruins are over,
*   And all the seasons of snows and sins;*
The days dividing lover and lover,
*   The light that loses, the night that wins;*
And time remember'd is grief forgotten,
And frosts are slain and flowers begotten,
And in green underwood and cover
*   Blossom by blossom the Spring begins.*
        'Chorus from "Atalanta"', Algernon Charles
                            Swinburne, 1837-1909

The purpose of this book is to provide entertainment and pleasure, not only by actually working the patterns but in reading about embroidery and deciding exactly what to do. In fact, I think that much of the enjoyment in needlepoint is in making up one's mind about which design to do, how the finished work will be used, and selecting the colours. The patterns are intended to offer ideas and inspiration for your own interpreta-

tive talents. It is not a book of rules telling you how to do needlepoint.

THE ARTISTIC IMPULSE

Humanity has always contrived to provide itself with goods whose end is to make life more practical and comfortable. We have also had an irres-

Topiary remains a favourite feature of the more formal English country house garden.

istible urge to enhance such objects with decorations. While a great many of these decorations have been religious in nature, others serve no better cause than that of the artistic impulse. Embroidery, the decoration of something using a needle and thread, has been with us during all these thousands of years.

The argument about what is 'craft' and what is 'art' is relatively new in terms of our long history. Some people feel that art has no end in mind except beauty or the perception of a new truth while craft is about an end product which, while perhaps beautiful, serves a practical purpose. Yet, without making any such distinction, we

The fringed petals
of Ehret's parrot tulip:
a triumph of botanical
naturalism in art.

admire the jewellery of Islam, the salt cellars of
Cellini, and a painting by Édouard Manet. Any
attempt at separating art from craft and declaring each 'different' in some way not only serves
little purpose, as far as I am concerned, but has
prevented many gifted people from undertaking
for themselves the creating of things which
satisfy their artistic impulse. Whether those
things are an embroidered jacket, a watercolour,
a footstool or a sculpture is irrelevant. We are
too eager in this age of the expert to decide what
is 'good' and what is 'wrong' when such judgements are, after all, a matter of personal taste.

More important, we seem all too ready to
leave such judgements up to the experts. For me,
'craft' or 'art' are simply words to describe the

carrying out of particular techniques on specific
materials that result in something reflecting the
vision we may have of what is represented, what
we want it to say about ourselves to others, or a
truth of living that we believe in. Thus, how you
embroider a flower may tell something about
how you see flowers and feel about them.

One of the most useful definitions, if one must
have definitions, in making some distinction between, say, the salt cellars of Cellini and the
painting of Manet, is to recognize that the distinction between what are termed 'fine arts' and
the 'decorative arts' to which crafts such as
embroidery belong, is ultimately a pragmatic
one. Such a distinction was unknown in antiqui-
ty and is foreign to most cultures other than the
Western one. The concept of fine art, with all its
associated mystiques, only became part of our
thinking during the eighteenth century. The decorative arts are thought to be those which
serve some useful purpose – but which are
prized for their beauty and quality of workmanship. The list is a long and familiar one involving
as it does the everyday objects of life: leather,
textiles, glass, paper, landscaping, photography,
jewellery, enamelling, toys, lace, embroidery
and gardening. These are just a few of the decorative arts.

CRAFT BOOKS
Craftsmanship means more than mere technical
virtuosity. It demands a profound understanding
of the materials and tools with which you work.
A bookbinder, for example, who has no sympathy for leather will probably not use it to best
advantage in rebinding a book. Similarly, an
embroiderer who cannot feel and appreciate the
difference in texture and colour reflection between silk and wool is unlikely to be able to
achieve many effects with either. The word 'art'
after all comes from the Latin *ars* or 'skill'.

There has been a proliferation of craft books
during the last twenty years which reflects the
increased leisure time available to most people
in the West. The increasing number of courses
and classes on a wide variety of crafts attests to
the fact that people are discovering the pleasure
and satisfaction that a craft like needlepoint can
bring to their lives. It also allows a person to

make something for themselves, their home, or as a gift for someone else. In an age which has seen such widespread distribution of machine-made goods, more and more people are coming to appreciate handmade things.

> *O happy season of the brink,*
> *When Nature seems to wait and think*
>   *And pays her last adieu;*
> *Then tossing wild arms to the sky*
> *She seizes Spring's embroidery*
>   *And decks herself anew.*
>   *Country Life,* Peter Leslie, 7 March 1908

Most craft books are little more than manuals of instruction. Some of these are excellent. The problem with them lies not so much in what is said about technique but in how well the instructions are communicated. It is for this reason that one of the easiest, most enjoyable and best ways of learning the techniques of any craft is from a master craftsman. In former times we might have been apprentices to such a person or, as children, we might have learned embroidery at school. Today we go to adult education classes, watch TV, utilize educational video recordings, or buy a craft book. In the final analysis the best craft book is the one from which *you* are able to learn.

A Word about Pride

There is a place in all good craftsmanship for genuine pride – pride in what we are doing and the carrying out of the skills with attention and care. To make something as well as you possibly can is an impulse that deserves the highest praise. This impulse, inherent in all humans since prehistoric days, invades many of our activities and certainly our craft work, and seems to be a desire for excellence. It is an impulse to make something beyond its mere practical purpose and beyond any financial reward. It is the distinction between mass-produced and crafted objects, for the first have a different ethic of adaptation to the market place and a built-in obsolescence. The craftsman's object has elements of pride and the intention to create durability in the aesthetic sense. The booming trade in handicraft shops and craft fairs certainly attests to the interest and preference of many people for handmade goods. From potters to embroiderers, crafts have entered a new era of appreciation and popularity, while the shoddy workmanship of many consumer goods has forced manufacturers to rethink design, quality control, and look again at what people really want to buy. For handmade crafts to blossom in the age of the throwaway is as odd a phenomenon as the growth of interest in real, natural foods in the era of fast-food.

When it comes to doing embroidery with pride in attention to detail, then time should cease its stressful role in our lives, mean something pleasant and be our servant for a change. When you are doing needlepoint, time should slip by unnoticed.

The American Tradition

While there have been many cultural influences from other countries which have helped to develop the style of decorative arts in the United States, the background historically for American embroidery is that of England. It started with the early colonial settlers who imported most of their consumer goods – and skills – from Europe. For such reasons, needlepoint in the United States is understandably biased towards the English embroidery tradition. In my opinion, while each enjoys its own modern development, the embroidery of the two nations remains very much related. Perhaps some of this is due to the long admiration each country has had for the other's interior decoration and furnishings.

I admire the vigour and sheer artistic simplicity of line and presentation in American Folk Art, including the dazzlingly artistic and technically skilled patchwork and appliqué work. Fortunately, the American Museum at Bath gives the British embroiderer a chance to see many examples of this fine needlework tradition.

> *Needlework is an art so indissolubly connected with the comfort and convenience of mankind at large that it is impossible to suppose any stage of society in which it has not existed.*
>   The Countess of Wilton in *The Art of Needlework,* 1840

New synthetic materials have provided an increasing challenge to many modern embroiderers and these are reflected in abstract and geometric needlepoint patterns, many of the most original and professional of which are destined for wall hangings in buildings whose stark modernity demands the restful respite of textile art to soften and warm the decor.

EMBROIDERY IN THE HOME

Embroidery is an ancient craft and, along with weaving, has been found to exist in the earliest recorded periods of human history. It was probably first used in the decoration of garments. At some point, wool was used to work stitches on coarse linen. Fabric was gradually covered and, since silk was too fine and fragile a thread for this purpose, wool became the natural choice. In this way needlepoint became the type of embroidery in which the whole of the background of fabric is worked with thread. Today, in some modern needlepoints, the entire canvas is not worked, but this is merely an artistic variation on an established form of embroidery. Indeed, a small picture done in needlepoint can sometimes look more attractive, when framed, if the background canvas is left exposed.

The domestic needlewoman over the centuries seems to have been fairly conservative in her choice of patterns for the various needleworks in her home. These may be grouped into bedhangings, chair-seat covers, pictures, cushions, wall-hangings, linens – and clothing. In England we are fortunate in having many needlepoint embroideries still in the houses and settings for which they were made.

There is no simple way historically to look at needlework because it does not fall automatically into distinct periods of time. Changes in taste and fashion come about slowly. While domestic sewing to make and repair clothing and linens is the foundation and purpose over the years of most needlework, embroidery is the decoration of a fabric with thread and, thus, an option that can be used or not as desired. Given even a little bright thread, embellishments of plain cloth usually take place and, hence, embroidery has always been an acceptable way of improving and enhancing possessions. Since Roman times at least, there have been professional embroiderers, both men and women, just as

there are today, except there were formerly a great many more of them to satisfy demand. Wealthy households might employ a permanent staff in charge of sewing and, while fancy embroidery was generally left to the 'artistic' hands of the mistress of the household, her maids might join her in the completion of a large needlework enterprise.

THE LONG HISTORY OF THE AMATEUR

Domestic sewing seems always to have been among a woman's duties in the home so there has probably never been a time or a culture in which women did not undertake some needlework. The presence of the amateur embroiderer is so powerful in the history of embroidery, particularly from the sixteenth century onwards, that this influence is widely present in the examples of work we see today and, certainly, in the choice of patterns that were used. These patterns may well have been designed and produced by professionals, but what was created was, to a large extent, dictated by the amateur needlewomen of the time – particularly since the resulting embroidery was usually destined for use in the home. In our own age, when the number of highly skilled needlewomen – whether professional or amateur – is small compared to the last century, we may forget how very talented amateur embroidery really is.

When we see examples of such work in stately homes or in museum collections such as those at the Victoria & Albert Museum in London or the Metropolitan Museum of Art in New York, we marvel at their skill, talent and execution. Practice made such perfection possible and time to practise was something many women then had available. The day of servants is past for most people, and children are no longer taught sewing and embroidery, domestic skills once deemed so vital in every woman's life.

EARLY EUROPEAN TRADITION

France, Spain, Italy and Germany all have more examples today of canvaswork embroidery before the eleventh century, but England does pos-

In spite of the highly idealized child, the flowers remain familiar favourites – pink hollyhocks and fat sunflowers.

sess some good examples from later periods. There is the Syon Cope dating from the thirteenth century in the Victoria & Albert Museum. Another example is the corporal case in Wymondham Abbey in Norfolk which is dated sometime in the fourteenth century. Other examples in the Victoria & Albert are a purse and two seal bags on a charter of 1319 and the Calthorpe Purse dated at about 1540. A number of early embroidered bookbindings still exist, and one of the earliest is the Felbrigge Psalter in the British Museum.

The lack of many examples of needlepoint from such very early centuries does not necessarily mean it was not generally done or in use. From Saxon times English embroidery was renowned and, in the thirteenth century, there was nothing to rival the work done for the church known as *Opus Anglicanum*. While these works were silk, gold and silver thread embroideries, it is difficult not to believe that needlepoint must also have been widespread. The existence of needlepoint bookbindings and purses must indicate that similar work was done for bench cushions and other items where the entire surface of the fabric needed to be covered. One example of early English needlepoint found abroad is the thirteenth-century English Orfrey preserved at Lyons in France, which has tent-stitch in its construction.

The tools of a craft often indicate its advance and, in the case of embroidery, it is the needle in those early days that exerted a great influence. We take for granted our carefully graded metal needles, but once bone needles were used. Those which have been found in Saxon remains are shaped and useful but not as easy to handle or as fine as metal ones. The Spanish made metal needles, and these were imported during the sixteenth century in small quantities. A German, Elias Crowse, in 1556, introduced the making of 'Spanish needles' into England. This led to a great increase in the popularity of embroidery.

There are many reasons for scholarly uncertainty about how much needlepoint was done in these early centuries. One reason is that the terms applied to work like embroidery and tapestry in the writings of the period confuse rather than clarify matters. For example, in records of the thirteenth century, it is difficult to discern between embroideries, brocades, damasks, carpets, coverings of furniture, velvets or tapestries. The latter was applied to pictorial hangings after about 1204 when the tapestry weavers of Flanders became famous for their work, but until about 1280 wall-hangings were usually fabric embellished with embroidery. After that time, with the adoption of the high warp in weaving, tapestry really superceded embroidered fabric as wall-hangings. It was Henry III who made decorative tapestry wall-hangings fashionable in England.

One item of early embroidery that was widespread but is no longer a part of normal everyday fashion is the glove. Gloves, like hats, are something that are rarely seen these days. There are still occasions when women wear gloves for fashion rather than as protection against the cold, but these are usually formal events like weddings or funerals. Once the little glove with its elaborate embroidery was high fashion and must have enhanced even the oldest or roughest female hand. From the time of Charlemagne to the end of the fifteenth century the glove was at its height as a symbol, and how and when it was used was carefully observed. That one item of dress basically designed to keep the hands warm should turn into such an instrument of custom tells much about our concern with manners. Here are just a few ways gloves were used in those days:

The glove was used as a gage to combat. To throw the glove at the feet of a person meant a challenge. This custom remained in use among gentlemen up to the end of the sixteenth century.

To strike with the glove was to offer an insult.

To give a glove was to entrust with a mission of confidence.

From the earliest times it was considered a great insult to address a person of high rank or to greet a friend without first removing a glove.

To offer a glove signified homage. A present of gloves was a favourite way of recognizing indebtedness.

Out for a stroll in the local park wearing a beautiful, if rather unsuitable, embroidered coat.

If a lover possessed gloves, it was necessary that he should pay special attention to the manner in which they were worn when paying court to his beloved.

Gloves were not worn by men or women when taking the hands of partners in the dance.

It was regarded as showing a great lack of reverence to enter a church with the hands gloved.

The act of picking up the glove of one's ladylove was a sign of deep devotion.

Gloves treated with poison were favourite gifts to one's enemies.

ANGLO-SAXON EMBROIDERY AND THE BAYEUX TAPESTRY

A high degree of skill and sophistication was reached during the Anglo-Saxon period in England. The stole and maniple associated with St Cuthbert which is in Durham Cathedral, and in a reasonable state of preservation, shows how fine the technique of the Anglo-Saxon embroiderers really was and that they must have been professional. One of the most famous embroideries in the entire world is the Bayeux Tapestry. This embroidered hanging of coloured wools on linen is over 230 feet long with laid and crouched work combined with outline stitches. It depicts vivid scenes from the story of the Norman Conquest of England. It is thought to have been commissioned by Odo, Bishop of Bayeux, for the adornment of his new cathedral dedicated in 1077. The museum in France where the embroidery is now kept has been set up for visitors from abroad with multilingual tapes explaining the story. It is a fascinating and splendid example of early embroidery.

EARLY MEDIEVAL EMBROIDERY

The work of professional embroiderers was encouraged by the Normans among their newly conquered subjects. Many of the embroideries of this period were worked in silver-gilt threads on silk. Most of the embroideries which remain are couched in a Romanesque style in which animals set in medallions, leafy scrolls and human figures dominate. By the end of the twelfth century the quality of English embroidery was already known on the European continent and there are a number of pieces in European collections.

During the first half of the thirteenth century the style of embroidery gradually became less rigid and many were executed in the simple brick patterns quite common at this time. The great period of religious embroidery in England called *Opus Anglicanum* began in the middle of the thirteenth century. English embroidery was held in high esteem and this is indicated by the Vatican inventory of 1295 where examples of *Opus Anglicanum* were listed more than any other type of embroidery. The work was sought after by kings and church officials all over Europe and many of the finest surviving pieces can be found in continental churches and museums. English embroidery was extremely costly as quantities of silver, pearls and semi-precious stones were used to adorn it. Most of this work was carried out in professional embroidery workshops in London.

Very few secular embroideries have survived from the Middle Ages. Such fragments as exist show that applied work and woollen embroidery were used as well as the richer techniques familiar in ecclesiastical embroidery. In about 1400 embroidered design began to reflect the naturalism which was contemporary in painting and architecture.

Daffodils
That come before the swallow dares, and take
The winds of March with beauty.
'A Winter's Tale', William Shakespeare,
1564-1616

During the fifteenth century the practice grew up of embroidering motifs separately and then cutting them out and applying them to silk or velvet grounds – a way of quickly producing a richly decorated textile. This was, to a large extent, in imitation of the expensive patterned Italian silk brocades and velvets which were in fashion at the time.

ELIZABETHAN EMBROIDERY

With the Reformation, the great tradition of ecclesiastical embroidery in England came to an end and in the early sixteenth century secular and domestic embroidery came into its own.

The Tudor monarchy brought to England very settled cultural and social conditions and a great increase in prosperity for many people. There was now time and money for the nobility and the prosperous landowners to pay more attention to the decoration of their houses as well as their persons. This interest, of course, led to much more embroidered embellishment of fabric. It was also during this time that the amateur began to produce work to compare with that of the professional embroiderer. During the Elizabethan period a whole new tradition of domestic embroidery came into being and for the very first time in England the work of the amateur was in many cases as good as that of the professional. Indeed, experts sometimes find it impossible to distinguish between the two. Lavishly embroidered court costumes were created; there were costumes for masques and heraldic embroidery was in great demand.

Pattern books were widely available and samplers of the period included elaborate designs of birds, fishes, flowers and plants as well as lace patterns. Many of the small motifs survive to this day, especially the flower, fruit and leaf sprays which remain perennial favourites. The fashion for including small insects such as caterpillars and butterflies was popular in Elizabethan and Stuart embroidery and the pattern books were full of them. Elizabethan embroidery favoured all-over patterns and most of the needlepoint was done on linen canvas with a mesh of 16 to 18 threads to the inch which produces very fine work. Little background space was left and the needlepoints were filled to overflowing with designs of flowers, fruits, human figures, birds and little scenes. Tent and cross-stitch now came into prominence for the first time. They were destined to remain the favourite stitch techniques of the amateur.

It is in the Elizabethan period that we see the growth of luxurious and magnificent needlepoint embroidery. The smaller pieces were almost certainly done by amateur needlewomen but the larger pieces – table carpets, hangings for walls and elaborate bed valances – are of such a consistently high standard of workmanship that many of these must have been ordered from professional embroiderers. Most such items were worked in wool and silk, mainly in tent stitch. There were cushions, wall-hangings, chest-tops, jewellery boxes, chair-seat covers, bookbindings, and a multitude of embellished finery to wear.

Although the earliest known English needlework carpet is ascribed to about 1550, the general practice of embroidering floor coverings did not become common until the eighteenth century. During the earlier periods – the sixteenth and the first half of the seventeeth century – carpets were made for table and chest coverings and were not in general use for the floor. After all, these beautiful works of art were expensive. However, of all the techniques of embroidery, needlepoint is the one which is most suitable for making a decorated floor covering because it locks the thread to the canvas and covers the entire fabric. It took the Great Fire of London in 1666 to sweep away many ideas about furnishings, including the widespread use of rush matting on floors, coupled with the introduction of new standards of hygiene to bring needle-made floor carpets into fashion.

A specialist kind of needlepoint called turkeywork appeared during this time. In this technique double strands of wool are passed through the canvas and knotted. The wool is then clipped very short to form a close pile, like that seen in Persian carpets, which was what turkeywork was trying to imitate as these imports had become very desirable for home furnishings.

In our day, it may seem odd that the Elizabethans should have spent so much time and effort in creating elaborate and expensive bed-hangings. But, in those days, the bedchamber was an important room. Guests were entertained there and so lavish decor was what wealthy and aristocratic householders wanted.

Mary, Queen of Scots, is one of the most famous names from this period and one which is closely associated with embroidery. Even today, four centuries after her death, this Queen excites curiosity. She led an energetic life and, although her embroidery output was less than

Ernest Llewellyn Hampshire's painting, overleaf, is that daydream of the romantic cottage garden.

has been believed, she managed to exert a great influence on domestic and Court decoration, and needlework in particular.

That other noblewoman of Mary's time, the Countess of Shrewsbury – or 'Bess of Hardwick' as she was known – in whose custody Mary remained for fifteen years of captivity, was also an accomplished embroiderer. The kings of Scotland had long employed male and female embroiderers, and Mary had no less than three upholsterers to provide her furnishings. One member of her staff was in charge of all the beds, curtains, tapestries and linen. This *valet de chambre* kept meticulous accounts of all these various textiles and objects so we know a great deal about what the Queen had in her household. For example, in 1561 she brought with her eleven beds from France, plus beds and linens formerly belonging to her mother, many of which were embroidered. Mary continuously commissioned new beds and hangings for herself, her household and her friends. It was during her lengthy imprisonments that Mary had the enforced leisure to do embroidery until, worn and her beauty gone, she was finally executed in 1587. There are many references in letters and memoirs to her embroidery activities, and two cushions at Hardwick have been identified as her personal work. Her cypher is on the Oxburgh Hall hangings in Norfolk. These are worked in fine tent stitch and a coarse cross-stitch.

Gather ye rosebuds while ye may,
  Old Time is still a-flying:
And this same flower that smiles to-day
  To-morrow will be dying.
      'To the Virgins, to make much of Time',
                    Robert Herrick, 1591-1674

Embroidery compositions frequently contained outlandish objects like elephants and exotic-shaped flowers. The realistic scale of these flowers, animals and fruit bowed to decorative values, and such works – for example a lion the same size as an apple – are surprisingly pleasing. Embroidered boxes, many done in needlepoint, could be delightful with a scene depicted on each side and on the lid. When you opened the box, you frequently found another little scene on the inside of the lid.

Elizabeth I also interested herself in embroidery and this was celebrated by the poet John Taylor in the words 'Whatever sorrows came and went she made the needle her companion still.' The Elizabethan embroiderers possessed an originality and technical skill that has rarely been surpassed.

NATURALISM IN THE SEVENTEENTH CENTURY

There were considerable changes in embroidery during the seventeenth century. At first canvas-work continued in much the same way as it had in Elizabethan times, but then the size of finished pieces became smaller and the designs simpler. Religious themes became fashionable. The strength of the canvas and the quality of the tent stitch were such that we still have many examples of the work to study and admire.

The Orient became a major influence during the latter part of the seventeenth century and this was reflected in the embroidery patterns. Floral designs became bigger, with flowers and leaves bolder and much more intricately shaded. There came about a considerable mixing of the two artistic influences of West and East, and embroidery patterns developed which consisted of interlocking abstract shapes worked in a variety of colours. Favourite flowers such as tulips, roses, honeysuckle and carnations continued to be done but the tendency in needlepoint patterns was towards greater naturalism. This reflected what was happening in the botanical paintings of the period.

SAMPLERS

Many beautifully worked samplers were done at this time. The embroidery was usually tent or cross-stitch. Earlier samplers were done as a permanent record of stitches, patterns and motifs which might be repeated on a later work. Later samplers which were signed and dated appear to have been the work of beginners as exercise pieces.

The eighteenth century samplers definitely showed a decreasing reliance on the old printed pattern books for their designs and there was a

Roses by Redouté continue to be among the world's most popular flower pictures.

Bengale Thé hyménée.

P. J. Redouté.

Victor.

A child of innocence and winter: William Dobson's
Christmas Roses.

possible to recognize in the birds, beasts and fishes of our patterns today a similarity with those of yesterday.

In the last few years the sampler has staged a comeback and there are now both charted as well as printed designs available. Antique samplers are much sought after and find high prices at auctions. It is easy to see why old and new ones are so popular – they make amusing pictures and can be personal. The alphabet in this book can be used to design and embroider a sampler of your own.

Fortunately, modern samplers do not contain the sad and mournful messages of so many of those in the last century, where admonishments were made or death was frequently mentioned. This was not surprising in an age when so few lived to adulthood and where disease, infection and endless pregnancies claimed lives very early on. It would have been surprising for any Victorian child to grow up without being involved in the loss of a beloved brother or sister or parent in the first ten, let alone first fifteen, years of their life.

There are many keen embroiderers on both sides of the Atlantic who do not regret the passing of the sampler because they are interested in using a variety of stitches rather than the familiar tent or cross-stitch in which many old samplers were done. One thing which modern educationalists and many embroidery experts decry is the fact that children in the last century sat working these samplers and doing fine stitches and being corrected about technique until they were accomplished needlewomen, and that this limited the children's own creative and artistic talents. I don't particularly agree with this decrying of the sampler and its use in teaching children to do needlework because it is at least an occupation where they can see the results of their own efforts. They have an opportunity to become accomplished at something that is manual and yet can be artistic. Colour is involved and the choice of materials to hand. I cannot believe that the schoolhouses of England or America in the nineteenth century were filled with unhappy little girls sitting doing sad samplers. On the contrary, perhaps they enjoyed themselves.

great interest in doing more natural-looking floral arrangements. It was in the nineteenth century that sampler-making became widespread and printed instructions for samplers appeared regularly during that century. While there had always been a great emphasis on technique, bringing embroidery so fully into the classroom certainly resulted in great attention to technical virtuosity. By the end of the nineteenth century, when women took up crochet and tatting and other forms of 'fancywork', they had no real need for samplers and these died out. Pattern books and dictionaries of needlework were published which catered for their new interests and explored the problems inherent in each of the skills with ample instructions. Samplers had outlived their usefulness.

It is, however, difficult to escape from some of the well-established motifs that you can see in eighteenth- and nineteenth-century samplers. The carnation frequently appears as does the strawberry. The lily is to be found as well. It is

BERLIN ARTWORK PATTERNS

The nostalgia that the British and the American people have had over the last decade for the Victorian era seems to be continuing. The modern and sometimes strident abstract patterns and bold use of colour that occurred in the 1920s and 30s seem to have disappeared and there has been a return to softer tones and patterns of more familiar things. Looking at the Victorians

Late in the year, chrysanthemums, holly and Christmas roses make perfect companions.

from the distance of time we admire much of their needlepoint and many of their ideas about comfort in the home, if not their moral dictates. One associates the Victorians with ornamentation, the combination of historic styles, great embellishment and their over-decoration of rooms. It is often forgotten that candles and gaslight make for shadows, and with dark furniture there was a need to brighten a room. What better than needlepoint in fairly dramatic colours such as the Victorians used.

During the latter part of the eighteenth century there was a general decline in the quality of embroidery in England and this is emphasized by the fact that the needlepoint being produced in France in the same period shows a marked superiority over any contemporary English embroidery. During this period there was the beginning of industrial wealth in England and by the nineteenth century wealth was more widely distributed among a confident middle class. These new rich men wanted to emulate the nobility and the wealthy landed class. Therefore, they preferred that their wives kept to a lifestyle similar to the one they admired in these classes. This set the scene for the popularity of Berlin Artwork patterns. It was to affect needlepoint design throughout much of Europe and America for many years.

It all began in 1804 when a seller of prints in Berlin issued a coloured needlework design on squared paper. Before this time there had been many patterns done on finely ruled grids, the lines of which were intended to correspond to the warp and weft threads of the linen on which you were working the needlepoint. The black squares were the stitches. Patterns such as this had been available since before the middle of the 1500s so in terms of the actual counted stitch pattern there was nothing new. The new aspect was that these were *coloured* which meant that anyone using them could not only copy the design square by square but also the colours chosen for the pattern. It was all so much more natural than the old black and white efforts.

These new coloured designs became extremely popular and another Berlin printer and bookseller named Wittich was encouraged by his wife to extend his business by making multi-ple copies of such patterns. Other publishers joined in what quickly became a financially remunerative business. Between 1810 and 1840, a period of only thirty years, no less than 14,000 different copperplate designs of this kind were produced for needlework. Russia, England, France, America, the Scandinavian countries and Holland imitated Germany in the production of these patterns, although Germany remained the largest exponent and exporter of the new style.

By 1842, in terms of the popularity of such patterns, first was Germany, second was Russia, third was England, and fourth was France, followed by America, Sweden, Denmark and Holland. The first three were by far the biggest users of Berlin Artwork patterns. The French never really took to them and they didn't become popular there. The number of people employed just to colour such designs in Germany was well in excess of a thousand.

At first these designs were worked in embroidery silk. Later, beads were introduced and, eventually, soft wool yarn became the principal material in which Berlin Artwork needlepoint was worked. It was at this time that aniline dyes were invented. These chemical dyes, which produce very bright, often garish colours, were produced in Gotha in Germany and the yarns dyed with them were sold in Berlin. This gave a name to the style of embroidery and, thus, it became known as Berlin Woolwork or Berlin Work and the patterns as Berlin Artwork.

In 1829 the readers of *The Young Lady's Book* were instructed in the new technique: 'Paper patterns, covered with black cross lines, to represent the threads of a canvas, and painted on the squares in the proper colours, may be bought at the worsted shops . . . The pattern is not to be tacked to the canvas, but merely placed in view as a copy.'

The making of these Berlin patterns was a slow business. Four different craftsmen were involved in the production. The most highly paid was the first craftsman. He made a master copy of the original pattern or picture by transposing

Here is everyone's idea of the true cottage garden – flowers, solitude, scenery and thatch.

it into a series of coloured squares. The largest of these, it has been estimated, consisted of over half a million squares. The second craftsman involved in the production of a Berlin pattern used a copperplate marked in squares of the same size and a symbol for each of the colours was put on this according to the master copy.

Most of us have seen such little hatch marks of 'x's' or dots or two dots on a charted pattern. They are codes for the colour of yarn that is to go in each square. The third craftsman printed the required number of copies of the engraving. The fourth craftsman coloured the squares by hand as indicated by those little coded symbols. I

have a few original Berlin Artwork patterns and, although the painting is very fine, you can still see under some of the light colours the coded symbols that were used. In 1842, Miss F. Lambert published a *Handbook of Embroidery*, and she declared that this fourth stage, where the squares were coloured, was work performed by

men, women and children. They were paid by the piece and the fastest earned the most money. A few coloured paper patterns were done in Vienna and these were mostly flowers, birds and arabesques. As to the colourists, a man could earn three shillings in a day and children sixpence to tenpence a day in piece-work. The designers were paid rather handsomely for the period – as much as forty guineas a design. Several copies of a chart were coloured at the same time, each square or line of squares being painted with a single stroke of a brush.

The German printseller, Ludwig Wilhelm Wittich, who first mass-produced Berlin patterns started with floral motifs which his wife had designed for her own embroidery. His patterns met with instant success, probably because the standard of the patterns and the quality of the reproduction were superior to what was already available for the embroiderer. What Wittich did was to take advantage of the organization that already existed for the production of hand-coloured charts on graph paper for the weaving industry in the production of tapestries. It must have been obvious that embroidery patterns for needlework could be represented in the same way as weaving patterns. Wittich was more than a printseller; he was a painter and an engraver of sufficient talent to be mentioned in several German reference books on art.

There was an earlier book on the history of embroidery entitled *The Art of Needlework*, edited by the Countess of Wilton and published in 1840, only two years before Miss Lambert's, and information in it about the background of Berlin Artwork patterns is much the same as in Lambert's book.

In England, Rudolph Ackerman sold Berlin Artwork patterns in his shop in the Strand in small numbers, and, in 1826, his son opened a similar business in Regent Street. There was also another shopkeeper, Mr Wilkes of Wilkes Warehouse, who was to become the largest importer of patterns and working materials in Britain.

In the early 1840s the Countess of Wilton noted that the new style in interior decoration

A realistic country garden with a clump of rhubarb – and apples and gooseberries to come.

helped spread this kind of ornamental needle-point since the fashion for furnishings where all the sofas and chairs should match changed to one where you had 'odd shaped articles of furniture'. This encouraged the working of a variety of embroideries instead of the 'constant occupation of a whole family – mother, daughter, cousins and servants – for years which indeed must have been completely wearisome' in the production of identical coverings for furniture.

Although there was much criticism of Berlin Artwork patterns during the early 1800s, embroiderers were still enthusiastic about them in the 1860s. There was criticism from clergymen about the limitations of such designs for ecclesiastical purposes. In view of the previous glory of English church embroidery, the clergy must have indeed felt there had been a decline. Architects, too, felt that the Berlin Artwork patterns lacked merit and were not serious art. But then, architects seem always to have set themselves up as arbiters of taste. In 1841 a compiler of a book of patterns for knitting, netting, crochet and Berlin Work with coloured illustrations, Mrs Henry Owen, put critics in their place by declaring that 'Berlin patterns serve to charm and amuse the minds of those ladies whose hours must be usefully as well as pleasantly occupied and give the finishing touches to the elegant furniture of their drawing rooms.'

Berlin Work was abundantly rich in roses and this flower was one of the most popular motifs with Victorians. There were rose gardens, rose-patterned dresses, hats, ribbons, wallpapers, and hundreds of variations on a rose theme in clothes and domestic objects – so it is not surprising that the rose dominates the floral patterns of Berlin Work.

If the Berlin Artwork patterns had stuck to floral designs or repeating motifs there might have been less criticism, but the reproduction of artists' paintings, such as those done by Landseer, were very popular during the Victorian era and Berlin Artwork patterns reproduced many such secular paintings as well as religious ones. Many of the patterns are of subjects which would not interest us today. It would be hard to imagine someone producing a series of Berlin Artwork patterns depicting the story of the life of

This original Berlin Artwork pattern is a typical one. The fancy motif at the bottom is how most border patterns were shown.

Joseph or of another saint and actually selling them. Although general-subject needlepoint pictures are easy to sell in antique shops today, those depicting religious subjects are avoided by traders.

THE HERITAGE OF THE ENGLISH GARDEN

If I were asked why I live in England, I would have to answer that it is because of the landscape – the hills and valleys filled with trees, the deep hedgerows adrift with cow-parsley and creamy meadowsweet, and the many gardens. Every corner seems to have something to offer: the parks with formal beds of flowers in cities like Cheltenham; the sweep of spring tulips and daffodils in Hyde Park; the tumbling honeysuckle on my neighbour's fence; another neighbour, hunched over at eighty, who can just be seen hoeing her vegetable patch through a frame of apple blossom; the river that runs under twisted willows and floods in winter; the moor filled with stars of white and purple thistles; the long hedge fragrant with roses, wild honeysuckle, elder flowers and damson in bloom that leads to the brook; the clumps of Rosebay Willow-herb to be gathered for my goats. With all of this, the making of a flower garden seems to be almost 'gilding the lily'. Yet gardens complement wild surroundings and in towns and cities where nature takes a back seat, the planting of small gardens, flowers in patio pots and in parks is necessary – not just for the sake of decoration but to help satisfy our spiritual needs.

Oh, Adam was a gardener, and God who made
him sees
That half a proper gardener's work is done upon
his knees,
So when your work is finished, you can wash
your hands and pray
For the Glory of the Garden, that it may not pass
away.
'The Glory of the Garden', Rudyard Kipling,
1865-1936

The English have loved flowers and gardening for so long that both are the subject of countless books and much myth. It is doubtful that William Shakespeare visiting Anne Hathaway at her parents' cottage in Stratford-upon-Avon would have found as many flowers and as much foliage as is growing there today. While there have always been flowers growing here and there about a cottage garden, the idea of a mass of flowers in a riot of colour is a fairly recent phenomenon.

Until the fifteenth century the cottage garden, as we know it today, hardly existed. Records of the time tell us that there were town gardens attached to small houses, particularly in London. In *The Life of Thomas à Becket* by Fitzstephen, he noted, 'On all sides outside the houses there are adjoining gardens planted with trees both spacious and pleasing to the sight.' There would have been apples and pears as a first choice and, certainly, a good planting of culinary and medicinal herbs. Monasteries seem to have been the dominant home of gardening before the fifteenth century. They kept extensive

enclosed herb gardens for the creation of medicines. In the countryside, people gathered wild food, such as strawberries, where it was allowed. The mass of people did not own land and tilled small strips rented from the lord of the manor. The cottages, too, were most often rented. The growing of flowers for beauty and pleasure could hardly enter the daily grind of living in those days. We forget that from dawn to dusk, ordinary folk spent their time – and still do in most of the world – obtaining food or necessary provisions such as firewood. What gardens they planted were put down to medicinal or culinary herbs such as garlic, leeks, onions, fennel and parsley. Knowledge of wild herbs and their use was widespread then and these would have been gathered from the surrounding land. Gradually, country people developed the scraps of land around their homes that became available to them. Fruit trees were added, then berry bushes such as gooseberries. A few flowering plants were grown, but more for their ability to enhance the flavour of food than for beauty. The pink was used to flavour and give fragrance to drinks, wine was made from the cowslip and the primrose, the seeds of the paeony were a condiment, and violets were used in salads.

The flowers listed as being used for culinary purposes by Jon the Gardener in his poem of 1440 were cowslip, lily, violet, periwinkle, red rose, white rose, foxglove, hollyhock, coriander and paeony. It was only natural that many of these should have become cottage garden flowers. Madonna lilies and dried rose petals were used for scenting damp and musty rooms. Wormwood, hyssop, lavender, sage and rue were just some of the herbs scattered over floors to make a room smell sweet. William Harrison, in his *Description of England* written between 1577-1587, reported that rich and poor alike grew all manner of herbs, roots and fruit including cucumbers, radishes, parsnips, turnips, carrots and cabbages. How little we have changed.

This rule in gardening never forget,
To sow dry and set wet.

Old Proverb

Gardening books often mention Thomas Tusser, who wrote *A Hundred Good Points of Husbandry* in 1557, because he gives long lists in bad verse of the herbs, flowers, vegetables and fruits that were grown and available in his day. He recommended dozens of seeds and herbs for the kitchen, some twenty plants for salads, twenty-one sorts of herbs to strew on floors, many fruits for the still-room, and about forty flowers for windows and pots which include many of today's favourites like columbines, carnations, roses, snapdragons, marigolds, lilies and hollyhocks. Tusser firmly put the farmer's wife in charge of this garden. She was to make certain it was planted, weeded and neat, while her husband was out working in the fields. This was, of course, in addition to all her other chores. One wonders when any of these women ever got time to do anything as decorative as embroidery – but they did.

There were many different beliefs about health and plants in those days and one theory based on astrology and planets found favour. In 1653, a herbal by Culpeper was published in which he advised people to consider which planet caused their disease, which planet governed the part of the body afflicted, and which planet governed the herb to be used. He declared that a cure is usually best effected by using a herb whose planet opposed the planet governing the disease – although sometimes diseases were cured by sympathy between the planets, bearing in mind that '. . . every Planet cures his own diseases, as the Sun and Moon by their herbs cure the eyes, Saturn the spleen, Jupiter the liver, Mars the gall and diseases of choler, and Venus diseases in the instruments of generation.'

It all seems terribly confusing and yet Culpeper's *Herbal* is still in print today. Just consider these relationships between your plants and the heavens, and be warned:

This basket of fruit by an unknown nineteenth-century artist would make a lovely needlepoint worked in silk. In this medium the fruits will have an appetizing sheen. An alternative would be to work the fruits and the basket in a variety of stitches in wool.

A TABLE OF PLANETS GOVERNING SOME OF CULPEPER'S 'HERBS'

Bilberry	Jupiter
Bramble	Venus in Aries
Cherry tree	Tree of Venus
Cowslip and catmint	Venus
Christmas rose	Saturn
Clove gillyflower (carnations)	Jupiter
Clover	Mercury
Gooseberry	Venus
Holly	Saturn
Honeysuckle	Mercury
Lily	Moon
Peach, pear, plum	Venus
Paeony	Sun
Poppy	Moon
Primrose	Venus
Red rose	Jupiter
White rose	Moon
Damask rose	Venus
Crocus (saffron)	Sun
Hawthorn	Mars
Vine and violet	Venus

By the early seventeenth century gardening had become a major pastime of the rich, and gardens were created for sheer beauty and delight. This was a time when fortunes were made and many people jumped from being poor to being prosperous and from there often to great wealth. The average cottage garden remained much as it had been – a patchwork of vegetables, fruit and herbs. Towards the end of that great century of change in England, John Worlidge in his *Systema Horticulturae* could write that there was 'scarce a cottage in most of the southern parts of England, but hath its proportionate garden, so great a delight do most men take in it'. Thus, the scene was set for the wide popularity of gardening with everyone whenever they had a bit of land. This created the personal and intimate landscape of England that we love today. When there was space for growing flowers, these too increasingly found their place. The fact that many were grown for culinary or medicinal use does not mean that the person who planted them did not also admire their flowers and fragrance – runner beans in flower look as handsome to me as a display of show-bench dahlias.

White currants, roses and red raspberries make an unusual collection, but one that could have been gathered from most Victorian gardens.

It was in the eighteenth century that the garden we romantically think of as 'the cottage garden', with its arches of climbing roses, its fences burdened with fragrant honeysuckle, and a path banked with a myriad of flowers winding its way to the front door, became a reality. Country folk did not create this image but followed the trend set by more sophisticated people – probably town dwellers – who romanticized country life then as much as they do now. By the end of the eighteenth century, buying country cottages, fixing them up and planting 'a cottage garden' which was deemed artistic in its simplicity was quite the fashion with the gentry. Great landscaped parks and most flower gardens and the walled acres of kitchen gardens continued to belong to the rich just as they do now. A staff of gardeners ensured that stately homes had a steady supply of fresh food and acres of charming gardens in which to ride or stroll.

THE SUBURBAN GARDEN

With the nineteenth century came the establishment of what we recognize as the suburban garden – usually a formal entrance, a drive, neat formal beds of annual flowers, often a conservatory for more exotic blooms, which were prized possessions and significant of the householder's financial status. The rear garden was given over to paths, more formal flowers and shrubberies,

and a few shade trees. Beyond, there was likely to be a fruit and vegetable garden.

Today, we seem to have successfully combined the cottage garden ideal and the practicalities of town living with its limited space. We have arrived at a mixture of styles and ideas which makes visiting someone else's garden such an adventure. Gardens are open to the public on an organized and national scale in Britain these days, giving hours of enjoyment to people, including those who have no space for a garden and must rely at home on a potted geranium on the window sill.

A little garden not too fine,
Enclosed with painted pales,
And woodbines round the cot to twine,
Pin to the wall with nails.

Let hazel grow, and spindling sedge,
Bent bowering overhead;
Dig 'old man's beard' from the woodland hedge
To twine a summer shade.

Beside the threshold sods provide,
And build a summer seat;
Plant sweet briar bushes by its side,
And flowers that blossom sweet.

John Clare, 1793-1864

The weather which the English constantly talk about is a true friend to their gardening endeavours. It is a temperate climate, with winters which are not too harsh and summers which are not too dry. It is the country where the perennial border is at its finest. Unfortunately these borders demand a lot of care, but when pink lupins stand up with azure delphiniums and the whole border bows and blows with colour and masses of flowers, it all seems worthwhile and one thinks 'this *is* the English garden.'

The natural affinity between the garden and embroidery is reflected in the way we live and both seem a compulsive decorative impulse. Whether ancient Romans or modern New Yorkers, we want the garden inside as well as outside where we live – roses on cushions, lilies on the bedroom curtains, knitted strawberries to

This gentlewoman must surely have a needlepoint of roses to accompany her bouquet of fresh ones.

wear. Nowhere else can we see our delight in this habit more than in the choice of patterns for embroidery over the centuries. Not satisfied with roses, apple trees, borders of herbaceous flowers, clumps of clove-scented pinks, flowers to pick and flowers to give away, and yet more flowers left in the garden to enchant us, we still want to embroider the same things in our needlepoint. One of the favourite flowers of all time in garden or embroidery must surely be the rose.

THE ROSE

The rose and the rosebud seem the very epitome of Victorian needlepoint and Berlin Artwork patterns. It is unusual to find such needlepoint flowers without at least one of them being a rose. It is easy to understand when you consider the long love affair generation after generation has had with this flower. The roses in many of these Berlin Artwork patterns are what we now fondly call 'Old Fashioned Roses' – ones such as the Moss Rose, the Cabbage Rose and the Damask Rose. Colours of roses in these earlier embroideries are red, pink, crimson, scarlet, deep red-purple, yellow and white. Sometimes the colours were deliberately changed from natural ones to those not found in nature but which are pleasing to the imagination – such as pale fawn roses with grey foliage or deep blue roses with accompanying blue foliage.

Some do put rose water in a glass and they put
roses with their dew thereto and they make it to
boile in water then they set it in the sun tyll it be
ready and this water is best. Also dry roses put to
the nose to smell do comforte the braine and the
harte and quencheth spirits.

Askham's *Herbal*, 1550

The rose, like so many other garden flowers, provides us with pleasure long after the summer ends. We can use rose petals in pot pourri, rose water as a cosmetic and in cooking, and, of course, rose-hip jelly is famous for its taste and high vitamin C content. I am always surprised by how many of the garden flowers such as the rose not only bring us beauty to enthral our senses and inspire us to poetry and song, but delight us in other ways long after the garden has fallen asleep for the winter.

IN THE GARDEN

What of the glory of trees? In selecting plants and flowers from the garden, I had to leave out trees, but I have included leaves, some from autumn and some from spring and, of course, the flowers have leaves as well as blooms. To me, a needlepoint of different leaves can be as attractive as one which contains flowers.

Other things besides trees, plants and flowers make a garden. There are hundreds of creatures, from birds and butterflies to spiders and bees – those friends who are busy pollinating so we have flowers and fruit and making honey which we may share.

While modern Western orthodox medicine seems to have turned its back on the beneficial uses of honey, ordinary people, in their continuing use of complementary medicine, have not. Honey continues to be used to treat burns and honey with lemon or whisky remains a favourite home remedy. If you drink too much alcohol, try two tablespoons of honey with

lemon juice and warm water – it speeds up the oxidation of alcohol by the liver.

The claims of cosmetic manufacturers for the beauty benefits of honey have probably been going on for as long as women have chosen to enhance their looks. Most of the famous names in modern cosmetics have incorporated honey into their products at some time.

Here is a simple recipe for cleansing the skin which you can prepare at home. Dissolve 2 tablespoons of quality honey in 1 pint (20 fl. oz) of warm water. Pat this mixture on your face and neck for at least 5 minutes. Rinse the skin with warm water to finish the treatment.

Terracotta pots, wooden troughs, urns, fountains, statues and all manner of objects are found in gardens. Some of them are surprisingly successful. When I first visited the studio of the British sculptress Barbara Hepworth in Cornwall, I was impressed at how well her massive stone and metal sculptures worked in what is a very small garden near the sea. You walk around the sculptures and they tower over you. You even walk through one of them. Yet Hepworth's artistic achievement is such that these sculptures do not oppress but enhance the garden and your enjoyment of it, all of them seeming right to the eye. In recent years garden centres have begun to stock a wider range of artificial stoneware, much of which correctly sited looks good in the garden. Georgian and Victorian gardens contained many lead sculptures and objects, but these are very costly today. Except for pots of flowers, most objects in the garden establish a tone of formality. Like the flowers you plant, the objects you choose to put in the garden are entirely a personal choice. As they say, 'One man's treasure is another man's trash.' But spare me gnomes, please.

Pretty pots of flowers were as popular in the eighteenth century as they are today.

CHOOSING YOUR PATTERN

A needlework enthusiast is very often also a gardener or a flower arranger because of her colour sense and the sheer excitement of participating in something growing into form and purpose, even if that purpose is for pleasure. I think it is the colour more than the shape or style of growing things which entrances us.

Choice of colour in needlepoint based on charted patterns is one of the creative features of this kind of embroidery. There are no limits on what colours you choose for a pattern. While I hope that you will like many of the colours that I have selected for the patterns in this book, I also hope you will decide in some cases that *your* choice is the right one. We no longer live in the days when Berlin Artwork roses had to be so many set shades of pink and a certain hue of green. We also do not need to be tied to 'artistic' concepts of what is right or wrong. There are no rights and wrongs as long as what you decide to use pleases you.

The use of primary colours such as red, yellow and blue makes for visual impact whether the pattern is abstract or a naturalistic one. As you study the embroideries and other folk art of the past, the range of colours used becomes simpler and more restricted. Vegetable dyes can, however, give a range of colours, many of which are far more subtle and pleasing than the same hue in chemically dyed yarns. These earlier embroideries were done with the strongest of the available colours – often dark brown, red, yellow and green. The use of a limited palette of colours has much to commend it. A brief study of the crafts of the Middle East, especially Iran and Turkey, will quickly impress you with the stamina and rich effects that can be obtained by the use of only a few colours. The same is true of early woven Coptic textiles from Egypt.

Don't forget that black and white are colours too in needlepoint. They can be dramatic and stand out. If you choose to work your patterns in one range of a single hue – say pink – then try adding one totally different hue – say a yellow-green. The effect is to enhance the colour range of the pink.

The patterns in this book are printed in as bright a colour as possible. Unfortunately artwork of this kind with an overlay of black grid lines cannot reflect exactly the depth and brightness of the original drawing. This is why the hand-painted Berlin Artwork patterns look so bright but no-one would sit in little rows to hand-colour such patterns today.

SOME COLOUR TERMS

The terms *hue* and *shade* are both used when referring to colours. Generally the term hue refers to the colour itself, for example red, while shade refers to the degree of red, for example scarlet or crimson. Sample cards showing the colours of yarns available can be bought from manufacturers. These are called shade cards. In a shop stocking yarns you can point to a colour and say, 'I want some yarn in *that* colour' and everyone will understand what you mean. If, however, you are using a pattern and it says to work a flower in different shades of the same hue, then you will understand what is meant and, in any case, you should use a shade card to check the colours with which you are working.

COLOURWAYS AND HOW TO USE THEM

On each page where a pattern appears, you will find a *suggested* colourways list. The colourways give numbers for both Appleton's Crewel Wool which is coded 'A' and for Paterna Persian Yarn which is coded 'PA'. The colours are grouped according to the major hues. For example, all the reds, pinks and oranges are under the heading 'Reds' while all the yellows, golds and ambers are under the heading 'Yellows'. If the colours are for a border then the word 'Border' will appear in the colourways. Thus the colourways might read like this: the name of the design, say 'Tulips'; followed by 'Flowers' and the colours and yarn codes; then 'Stems and Leaves' followed by the colours and yarn codes; then 'Border' followed by the colours and yarn codes. Colourways are also given for small patterns in the book unless they are obviously the same colours as the large pattern design. Do remember that yarn manufacturers can and do change their ranges, adding and subtracting shades and can also change the code numbers. If you buy an Appleton or Paterna shade card every few years you will always have correct yarn codes to hand.

When studying a pattern and noting the colourways, consider the effect the pattern is likely to produce when it is worked in wool. For example, the pattern 'Summer Time' is a mass of flowers that would have seemed familiar to any Victorian. The mixture of such dissimilar flowers – some even only marginally blooming at the same time – is typical of many Berlin Artwork patterns. The heavy red and purple colours along with careful delineation of such flowers as lilies, combined with stylized rendering of some of the other flowers, is also usual in such patterns. The prominence of an exotic like the passion flower is also traditional. If this bouquet pattern were done in pastel shades, then the finished effect would not seem Victorian but much more modern.

'Hot' and 'cold' exist in terms of how we see a particular set of colours. For example, I consider that the pattern 'Lilies' is hot because it has lots of primary colours such as red combined with bright yellows, and only a few colours at that. The stripe of the design is bold and underscores the hot qualities of the colours used. On the other hand, the winter pattern called 'Snowflakes' is cold, with its winter blues and stark whites.

Again, the colourways I have suggested are just that – suggestions – and I hope you will decide for yourself what colours please you best. After all, one of the nicest things about wandering in any garden is that each of us sees the flowers differently and the beauty and joy of our senses, while often shared, is always unique to ourselves.

How to Use the Patterns

Setting out to tell someone how to use these patterns makes it all sound terribly difficult – as if there were something to *learn* before one could use them. This is just not true. Whether you are a beginner or an advanced needlepoint embroiderer, elements of the classroom and the traditional admonishments of the embroidery craft book have no place here, and I hope I have avoided as much as possible making anyone think differently.

Look up some of the numbers in the colourways in a shade card of the yarns you plan to use. See if they seem right to your eye. If not, choose a

few others. Next, buy the yarn. The size of the canvas mesh and the total area of the finished work will dictate the amount of each colour you need. If need be, take the patterns with you to the embroidery supply shop where you can get help in working out the amount of yarn you will need. Do remember that for the background you should buy enough all at once, as any variations in the manufacturer's dyeing between lots of yarn will show up. In working small flowers and leaves, it doesn't matter if you have to buy more yarn of a particular colour. Variations in shade will enhance rather than detract from your embroidery.

Twelve Useful Hints

As this is a book of needlepoint patterns and not a manual of instruction, here are just a few useful hints – but ones that will always help make for good end results.

1 Wash your hands before beginning your work.
2 Have enough light. Daylight is best but lamplight is fine as long as it is strong and directed onto your work.
3 Clean your glasses if you wear them.
4 Sit in a comfortable chair.
5 Use good needles and clean, sharp embroidery scissors.
6 Buy the best quality canvas you can get, preferably polished cotton.
7 Start at the centre of each pattern and work from there.
8 Work the pattern first, the background last.
9 Keep less than 18 inches (45 cm) of wool in your needle at any one time.
10 Try to keep the tension of your stitches even. Do not pull the wool too tightly.
11 Keep the back of the work free of knots.
12 Relax.

Using Part of a Pattern

There is no reason why you should not use just part of any of these patterns. For example, use two butterflies and some leaves from the 'Butterflies' pattern or just a few cherries from 'Cherries', or the border only from 'Forget-me-nots'. Do the strawberries as a repeat without the rabbit or work just the rabbit from the 'Rabbit in a Berry Patch' pattern.

WORKING MEDIUMS

Needlepoint is done in the mediums of wool, silk or cotton yarns on canvas. The canvas may be of linen, hemp, polished cotton or plastic. Try to buy the very best canvas. Do not pay good money for any that contain irregularities.

Basically there are two kinds of embroidery canvas, the single thread canvas, sometimes known as mono, and the double thread canvas which used to be known as Penelope canvas. The mesh of the canvas is the number of threads to the inch. These vary from as fine as 32 threads to the inch up to the very coarse canvas used for rug-making which may have only 4 threads to the inch.

The number of threads (or holes) to the inch determines the size of the finished pattern. The smaller the mesh, the smaller the design. The larger the number of threads to the inch, the larger the finished design. Some people count the stitches in following a pattern, others count the 'holes' on the canvas. Do whichever seems to work best for you.

If you have not done needlepoint before from a charted pattern such as the ones in this book, then you might be confused about the pattern grid count, which is 10 squares to the inch, matching your canvas mesh. Whether you choose to do your needlepoint on a canvas of 10, 12, 14, 16 etc. stitches to the inch, it will still match up with the pattern. Here is why: you do exactly the same number of stitches when you work any mesh size. The pattern will simply work out to be smaller or larger overall. *Simply do one stitch for one coloured square of the pattern.* What you are counting as you work are the number of squares which stand for stitches and *not* how many there are to the inch whether it is on the pattern or on your canvas.

Canvas comes in various widths and it is necessary when you are purchasing it to state the quantity, the width and the mesh required. When deciding the correct mesh to use for the design you want to do, it is necessary to have a reasonably clear idea of the fineness of the detail that you want. The smaller the mesh, the finer the detail will be of the pattern. The piece will also wind up being smaller in the total area it occupies.

Needles should be clean and blunt. If they become sharp in use, discard them and start with a new one.

SAMPLE STITCHES

During the Victorian age and until just after the First World War, needlepoint was usually done in either tent stitch or cross-stitch.

Eight stitches are illustrated to remind you how they are done. Below each stitch illustration is a caption which tells you how to do it. The patterns in this book are designed with the use of either tent stitch or cross-stitch in mind. The large number of small stitches of one colour and the non-repeating elements of most of the designs preclude the use of most other stitches. These two stitches are the traditional ones for doing this type of counted pattern. One of the stitches illustrated, tramé, is done only if you are working in tent stitch over a double thread canvas, so that your stitches cover the canvas and it doesn't show through.

A VICTORIAN CROSS-STITCH

In Berlin Artwork the cross-stitch was usually worked in a fashion which gave a very neat, bead-like effect. It is worked over two single threads or one pair of double threads. This stitch covers the canvas as well as most methods of working cross-stitch but it covers across rather than down the reverse side of the canvas. Anne Dyer, founder of the Westhope Craft College in Shropshire, England, and a leading British craftswoman, did considerable research to discover the technique of this stitch. She supported her study of original Victorian Berlin Artwork cross-stitch by later finding published evidence of the stitch in a 1903 manual of instruction. The stitch appears to have been dropped from general use about 1920 but is worthy of revival.

KINDS OF YARN

Needlepoint can be worked in any kind of yarn except the softest baby knitting yarn which pulls apart and breaks. However, the two yarns with which I work and which I find the best are Appleton's Crewel Wool and Paterna Persian Yarn. The colourways given in this book are for these two yarns. Appleton's offers an amazing range of

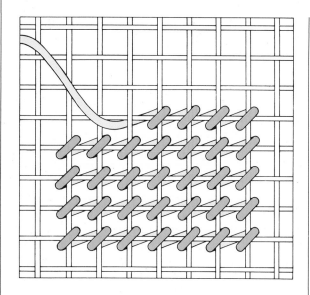

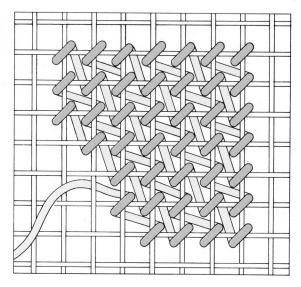

Tent Stitch or **Petit Point.** This stitch is worked on single thread canvas, in rows from right to left, each stitch over one crossing of the canvas, as seen above.

Tent Stitch or **Petit Point** over a large surface is done in diagonal rows, alternately up and down. The diagram shows the upward and downward workings.

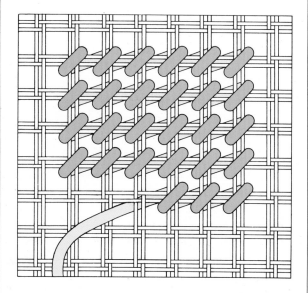

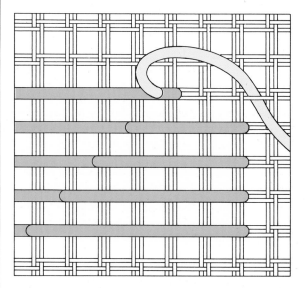

Gros Point, another form of Tent Stitch, is worked in the same way as Petit Point but over two threads in height and width, usually on double thread canvas in which case go over a pair of threads.

Tramé works best on double thread canvas. It is useful with Half cross-stitch. Use the same colour yarns for tramé that you will use over it. Working from side to side, take a long stitch and anchor it with a small back stitch over one mesh. Vary the length of the stitches, otherwise a ridge will appear.

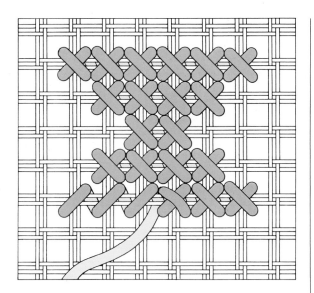

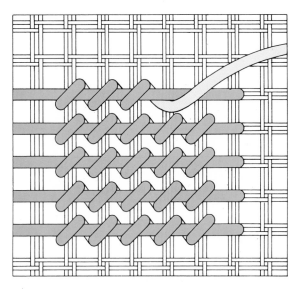

Cross-stitch can be worked in several ways. The simplest is worked in two rows. The first row is done from left to right. Then the journey is made back crossing each stitch to form the second row and complete each stitch.

Half cross-stitch is worked in rows from left to right and over two threads in single canvas and a pair of threads in double canvas, and over a laid thread (tramé) if the stitches do not sufficiently cover the canvas.

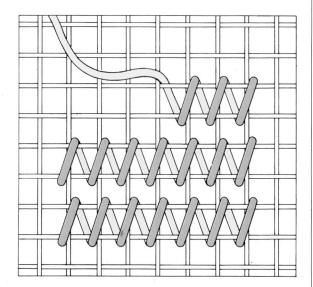

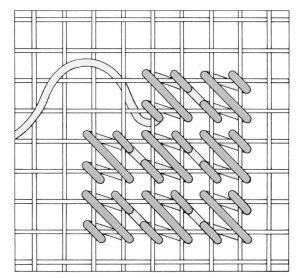

Gobelin Stitch, of which there are many variations, is often used for backgrounds. It goes over more threads in height than in width. It is normally always done on single canvas.

Mosaic Stitch is a neat, square stitch which in effect resembles a Cross-stitch. It is useful for background and for shading. Each stitch consists of three diagonal stitches worked over two horizontal and two vertical threads of canvas on single canvas or pairs on double canvas.

shades in any hue you could possibly need. Paterna also offers an extensive choice of shades. I find Appleton's colours have great subtlety and can be used to imitate older needlepoint embroidery colour schemes while Paterna colours are bright and clear with a deep intensity. There is a difference in strand count for different sized mesh canvases between the two types of yarn. Here are two charts to help you determine how many strands of Appleton's or Paterna yarn you need for the canvas mesh stitches to the inch you are going to work.

APPLETON'S CREWEL WOOL

Canvas	Tent Stitch strands	Cross-stitch strands
18 single mesh	2	–
16 single mesh	3	–
14 single mesh	3	–
13 single mesh	3/4	–
12 single mesh	4	–
12 double mesh	4	2
11 double mesh	4/5	2/3
10 single mesh	5	–
10 double mesh	5	3
9 double mesh	6	4
8 double mesh	7	5
7 double mesh	8	6

PATERNA PERSIAN YARN

The yarn comes as three strands loosely twisted and these can be easily separated. This table shows the number of appropriate strands.

Canvas	Vertical or Horizontal Stitches	Diagonal Stitches
18 single mesh	2	1
14 single mesh	3	2
13 single mesh	3	2
12 single mesh	3	2
10 single mesh	4	3
5 single mesh	12	9

ESTIMATING YARN AMOUNTS

It is difficult to give exact estimates of the quantity of yarn required for working a particular area as the various different meshes of canvas mean a different amount of wool. It is therefore best if, when buying the wool, you discuss with the shop the size of the canvas and the size of the mesh. If there are a great many threads to the square inch of the canvas and therefore a great number of stitches, the work is often referred to as *petit point*. On the other hand, if there are very few stitches to the inch then the resulting embroidery is often called *gros point* or, in the United States, *quick-point*. The only difference between these two types of needlepoint is in the scale of the canvas and the stitches. Both are needlepoint.

THINKING AHEAD: THE END PRODUCT

How is your needlepoint to be used?

Worked needlepoint canvas is nothing more than a fabric and can be used wherever a thick and stiff fabric would work. It serves as upholstery, around containers from wastepaper baskets to luggage and handbags, as a covering for floors or tables; it can also be used in terms of garments to wear, particularly as a vest or on the back of a jacket, bearing in mind how stiff the end fabric is.

CHOICE OF PATTERNS

It was difficult to choose which flowers and leaves to include among the patterns for this book. The English garden is such a rich jewel box of colour and shapes and brilliance throughout most of the seasons that it was hard to make a choice. From a technical standpoint the patterns were first drawn on graph paper in colour and these were then repeated in finished artwork for the book. If you feel that you like part of one of the patterns but not another section of it, or you want to try your own hand at creating a pattern, then all you do is get some graph paper and some coloured pencils and set to work. Remember each square represents a stitch. In order to create shadows and shading, and to turn leaves and petals as they actually grow and not have the pattern turn out 'flat' is tricky, but the right effects are achieved with experience.

The patterns in this book fall into several categories. First, there are what I call *Natural Patterns*, like 'A Lady's Bouquet', which attempt to imitate as closely as possible the actual flowers, stems and leaves found in the garden. Second are *Stylized Patterns* like 'Last Bouquets', in which the plants or flowers and leaves, while representing the actual thing, adhere closely to the overall shape rather than attempting to bring much detail of the living flower into the pattern. Then there are the *Repeat Patterns* like 'Cherries', where a single motif is repeated throughout the pattern to give an overall effect. In a repeat pattern, you can continue it over as large a canvas as you want, and this type of pattern is especially good for needlepoint to cover chair seats or upholster soft furnishings.

Many of the patterns in this book have *Borders* and *Frames*. If you like, you may leave them off the pattern in which they appear or you can use them for another needlepoint work – not necessarily one from this book. Borders and frames are fun to work and give a needlepoint a finished look. Try making up a border of your own from a few of the colours in one of the patterns you choose to work. Turning corners with borders and frames can be tricky. It is best to start in the middle of the top of the border or frame and work carefully to one corner, keeping strict count of your stitches as you go. Then go the other way from the middle to the opposite corner. From that point onwards it is easy just as long as you count the stitches correctly. Borders need this attention, just as geometric or repeat patterns do. When you are working leaves or flowers a stitch either way does not matter, but in repeats, borders and geometrics the object is to start and finish exactly where intended.

There are many small patterns of flowers, fruit, birds, butterflies and a dragonfly scattered throughout the patterns and these I call *Small Designs*. Such patterns which include motifs like the honey bee can be repeated over a canvas, done separately or, in the Elizabethan style, done a number of times over one canvas and joined together solely by the background colouring.

Finally, there are what I call *Backgrounds within Patterns*, such as the lattice or trellis effect in the pattern for 'Nasturtiums' or the one for 'Buckfast Cyclamens'. If you like one of these trellis effects, why not use it separately for a needlepoint without the central motif? Another way that is nice if you are doing several cushions for a room is to do one of the patterns, say of 'Nasturtiums', as it is shown in the book. Then do a needlepoint for another cushion of just the trellis effect and the border. Backed with the same fabric and edged alike, the cushions will make a pleasing pair.

A WEALTH OF ALTERNATIVES

In working these patterns you will probably use wool which is the usual thread choice, but you may also work the patterns in silk, mercerized cotton, or even in beads – which would mean one bead per coloured square as if it were a stitch.

PICKING THE PATTERN YOU WANT TO EMBROIDER

The patterns in this book are based on the type called Berlin Artwork patterns in that they are graphed in colour. Each small square represents one stitch. They are very easy to use. Simply count the stitches as you go along. If there is a line of red squares, say seven squares, then do seven red stitches, and carry on in this manner.

Do not let various needlepoint terms and definitions stand in your way. For example, *Petit Point* in the United States usually means either English *Gros Point* or *Petit Point* on 18 inch canvas or finer, while *Gros Point* or *Quick-point* in the United States usually means either English *Gros Point* or *Petit Point* on 16 inch mesh or coarser. (Now you see why I say you should get on and pick a pattern you like.)

Marry your children, sack your servants, forget your enemies, remember your friends, enslave your admirers, fatten yourself – and all will yet be well.

Walter Raleigh to Mrs Dowdall

Leisure is needed when making your design choice. Don't rush it. Sit down in a quiet place. Passive energy is what you need, for the decision is one you will live with for a long time. Look at the patterns. Study the ones you like best. Then let them stew in your mind, perhaps propping the book open at your choice so you can spot it as you pass. Let it catch you in *all* your moods.

A NOTE ON GEOMETRIC OR ABSTRACT PATTERNS
This book is not about geometric and abstract patterns which really lend themselves to a greater variety of stitches. However, geometrics can make excellent backgrounds for many of these patterns whether worked in cross-stitch or tent stitch or not. The regular mesh canvas used in needlepoint is perfect for geometric designs and is easy to count. Unlike the patterns for flowers and leaves, where a few stitches one way or the other will hardly matter, in geometric designs the formality of the repeat demands exact repetition of each part of the design. Otherwise you end up with a crooked line or a misshapen block of colour – for example, the rose in the pattern 'Rose Geometric' might not fit completely into where it is supposed to go. Then you will have to spend many hours ripping the yarn out and starting again. Once I did a 'free-hand' geometric repeat based on a Persian carpet but made it up as I went along. I must have ripped out and redone this needlepoint five times before I finally got lines to match up and the repeat to count out correctly.

Consider the wide range of geometric patterns all around you: hexagons, octagons, combinations of stars and rosettes, squares, pentagons – shapes familiar and odd. They all add up to a fresh look for your needlepoint. Many work successfully as part of a design of flowers and leaves or as a background. I have embroidered flowers and then made the background alternating light and dark blue checks.

While the geometric pattern is a formal one, it can serve as the 'lift-off' point for doing very abstract designs where one loses the formality of repeated set lines and moves into the realm of shadow, colour and texture. This is very much the dominion of certain modern schools of needlepoint which seek originality of stitch use and design in an attempt to create works deemed 'art'.

ALPHABETS
I have included an *Alphabet* in upper and lower case. So many needlepoint embroideries are destined for special gifts and putting in a person's name or a familiar, wise or humorous saying can add greatly to such a needlepoint. Use whatever coloured yarns you like to work the alphabet. It could be used as it is for a framed picture, or for repeating in needlepoint your favourite poem, or for one of the sayings or poems in this book. I hope that when you are finishing the background of your needlepoint, you will put in your initials and the date. Needlepoint work lasts for many generations and you contribute to scholarship and future interest in embroidery by putting in the date. Just think how many times you have picked up an old piece of needlepoint and wished you knew when it had been done – or found a needlepoint among your family possessions and wondered if it was your grandmother or her sister or some other relative who worked the embroidery.

OLD SAYINGS AND HOW TO USE THEM
One thing that amused past generations was to repeat old sayings – sometimes to admonish, sometimes to make fun, and sometimes because old folk sayings have a familiar ring of truth about them. I have selected just a few out of the many thousands that are part of the British and American heritages, many of which are common to both countries. They can be added to a pattern either at the bottom or the top, used as a little sampler, or worked with a surrounding border – with a flower motif worked at either end of the saying.

One of the best sayings is some words of William Shakespeare from *Troilus and Cressida* that serve to remind every embroiderer to continue in the pursuit of excellence in their craft and in the exploration of their talents.

Perseverance, dear my Lord,
Keeps honour bright: to have
    done, is to hang
Quite out of fashion, like
    a rusty mail
In monumental mockery.

A basketful of *English Garden Embroidery* patterns – Pears, Tulips, Rabbit in a Berry Patch, Rose Geometric and A Lady's Bouquet.

A Sampler Alphabet

Old sayings or maxims always seem familiar. They remain with us from generation to generation simply because they seem to contain some truth about life that most of us recognize. I like putting them in designs for they amuse and, sometimes, give pause for thought. The sayings on old samplers are rather long and often melancholy so I decided against including any of them here. If we want a saying to suit an embroiderer, this one seems appropriate: 'Haste makes waste.'

Time passes away, but sayings remain.

A bird in the hand is worth two in the bush.
A bird is known by his note, a man by his talk.
A fool and his money are soon parted.
A friend in need's a friend indeed.
A good conscience is a soft pillow.
A grain of prudence is worth a pound of craft.
A man is known by the company he keeps.
A mewing cat is never a good mouser.
A pig bought on credit grunts all the year.
A rolling stone gathers no moss.
Beauty without virtue is like a rose without
    scent.
Be reasonable and you will be happy.
By the street of 'By-and-By' one arrives at the
    house of 'Never'.
Custom is the plague of wise men.
Don't cry 'Holloa' till you're out of the wood.
Early to bed and early to rise, makes a man more
    holy, more healthy, wealthy and wise.
Economy is no disgrace; it is better living on a
    little, than to outlive a great deal.
Empty vessels make the most sound.
Enough is as good as a feast.
Experience cannot be bought with other
    people's money.
Experience is the best teacher.
God does not pay weekly, but pays at the end.
God is a good worker, but he loves to be helped.
Good to begin well, better to end well.
Happy is he that is happy in his children.
He lives long enough who hath lived well.
He who sows brambles must not go barefoot.
Idleness is the devil's snare.
If fools did not go to market, bad wares would
    not be sold.
Industry is the parent of fortune.

Kindness, like grain, increases by sowing.
Labour has a bitter root, but a sweet taste.
Love me, love my dog.
Love rules without a sword.
Man proposes, God disposes.
Marry in haste and repent at leisure.
Ne'er cast a clout till May be out.
Nothing is more precious than time.
No use crying over spilt milk.
Old friends are best.
Old trees are not to be bent.
Patience is a plaster for all sores.
Patience overcomes all things.
Praise the sea but keep on land.
Pride goes before a fall.
Riches breed care, poverty is safe.
Right mixture makes good mortar.
Roses and maidens soon lose their bloom.
Sleep without supping and wake without owing.
Soft words butter no parsnips.
Speak little and well, and they will think you
    somebody.
Speak the truth and shame the devil.
Spending your money with many a guest,
    empties the kitchen, the cellar, and chest.
Take the world as it is, not as it should be.
The devil sets his foot on the blackberries on
    Michaelmas Day.
The early bird picks up the worm.
The shortest answer is doing the thing.
The tongue cuts where the teeth cannot bite.
The truest wealth is contentment with a little.
Today must borrow nothing of tomorrow.
When the fox preaches, take care of your geese.
Wise counsels seldom prosper.
Words instruct, examples persuade.

Oh, to be in England
    now that April's there,
And whoever wakes in England
    sees, some morning, unaware,
That the lowest boughs and the brushwood sheaf
Round the elm-tree bole are in tiny leaf,
While the chaffinch sings on the orchard bough
    In England – now!
                    'Home-Thoughts, from Abroad',
                        Robert Browning, 1812-1889

SPRING

Spring may often be late but she can never arrive too early. Like a shy child, she peeps at us with yellow crocuses, tiny aconites and fragile snow-drops, then steps into full view with violets, primroses, daffodils and, if we are lucky, bluebells in the wood and cowslips in the meadow. From shyness to showing-off takes only a little while and we are soon treated to hyacinths, narcissi, lilac, the perfume of wall-flowers, branches of almond blossom and the enamelled blue flowers of forget-me-nots. This is the England of the poet's dream.

The first season of the year begins the long adventure into colour for the needlepoint work-er. Winter's limited palette is left behind and the primary colours of red, green, blue, yellow and orange appear in hues that range from bright scarlet to sky blue. It is easy for the embroiderer to fall into the trap of undertaking too many different kinds and shapes of flowers and leaves when confronted by such an array. I have tried in the first section to balance the designs between overall repeats of a single theme, such as for May blossom and for cherries; the geometric effects of designs such as for trellis-work and wrought-iron; and the more naturalistic flower patterns such as for tulips. Finally, there is a bouquet as detailed as any Berlin Artwork pattern of the Victorian era. My own choice would be to begin with the simple snowdrop in its frame to make up into a small cushion.

Now is the time when decisions about what flowers to embroider are matched by activities in the garden: deciding what summer annuals to grow; tidying up the debris of winter; discover-ing what damage late frosts have done; and con-sidering what new plants and shrubs to plant. Through the centuries, the English garden has welcomed new plants from around the world and the choice is now so large that the garden can maintain colour and flowers without a break between spring, summer and autumn. Many cottage garden plants are perennials and re-quire little attention except occasional weeding, provided you give them an annual dressing of fertilizer. If you thought about putting in some new roses and missed doing it in autumn, you can try again now. The shrub roses claim my affection and while they don't last long, their heavy heads and perfume bring to life many old needlepoint embroideries, especially those featuring fat cabbage roses.

Spring is a time of activity, all centred on the renewal of love, birth, good health and growth – a time when old men feel they will last another year and the young are dizzy with vitality. The garden, left to its own devices, soon collects weeds and wild plants to offer man and beast plenty of stuff for tonics and decoctions for good health. Cottage gardens have long been a source of this herbal or 'green' medicine and, today, with the growing recognition of the advantages of complementary medicine and the value of traditional remedies gentle to our bodily sys-tems, sales continue of old herbals with their recipes.

For the embroiderer, a study of illustrated herbals will pay dividends not simply as a means of learning about herbal teas and other prepara-tions that are good for you but for studying the

A cluster of primroses.

pictures of the plants. These were the basis of much embroidery in Elizabethan times and, for this reason, the embroideries often show not just bloom, leaf and stem but the roots as well, in a style exactly duplicating those seen in the popular herbals of the day.

I have seen foreign flowers in hot houses of the most beautiful nature, but I do not care a straw for them. The simple flowers of our spring are what I want to see again.
    John Keats (1795-1821) in a letter to James Rice

These sentiments by Keats are not felt solely by the English. People around the world long for the flowers, plants and colours of a landscape intimate to their memories, like a garden of their childhood. It is little wonder that, resident in foreign places, we may dream of a familiar rose, the new leaves on a certain village oak or the

sweetness of a strawberry. At no time of the year do these feelings seem to run as strong as they do in the spring. In our mind we can see the flowers of columbines, clematis, fritillary, violets, snowdrops, crocuses, narcissi, tulips, peonies, lupins, poppies, primroses, cowslips, pansies, forget-me-nots, cornflowers, daffodils, lilac and wisteria. And, joining these, the first bumble bee, the lucky ladybird that drops from winter hiding back into our lives, the mornings filled with bird chatter, and house martins dipping in the sky like stringless kites. Then we can sing again that praise of old, 'The Song of Songs':

For, lo, the winter is past,
The rain is over and gone;
The flowers appear on the earth;
The time of the singing of birds is here, and
The voice of the turtle is heard in our land.

While we may embroider flowers in colours which approximate to the real thing and interpret how we see the plant, the one thing we cannot do is to add fragrance – the perfumes that tell us more than anything that life is in the very air of our gardens. Smell is, after all, the most faithful of all our senses: 'The only one,' Colette wrote, 'that will not compromise.'

There is no time like Spring,
When life's alive in everything,
Before new nestlings sing,
Before cleft swallows speed their journey back
Along the lifeless track –
God guides their wing,
He spreads their table that they nothing lack –
Before the daisy grows a common flower,
Before the sun has power
To scorch the world up in his noontide hour.
    'The First Spring Day', Christina Rossetti,
    1830-1894

There are significant reasons why such flowers as violets and roses, heavy with scent, were highly esteemed over so many centuries. Sweet breath is supposedly a mark of a saint in Christianity, for fragrance was considered God's breath on earth and, thus, holy and healing. Sweet scents are so much a part of the pleasure of our senses it is not surprising that ideas of paradise should always include our most favoured scents and high among these would be the violet. The Garden of Eden was a lost paradise of beautiful scented plants, indeed the perfect flower garden.

Now the lusty spring is seen;
  Golden yellow, gaudy blue,
  Daintily invite the view:
Everywhere on every green
Roses blushing as they blow
  And enticing men to pull,
Lilies whiter than the snow,
  Woodbines of sweet honey full:
    All love's emblems, and all cry,
    'Ladies, if not pluck'd, we die.'

Yet the lusty spring hath stay'd;
  Blushing red and purest white
  Daintily to love invite
Every woman, every maid:
Cherries kissing as they grow,
  And inviting men to taste,
Apples even ripe below,
  Winding gently to the waist:
    All love's emblems, and all cry,
    'Ladies, if not pluck'd, we die.'
      'Love's Emblems', John Fletcher, 1579-1625

Almost all the flowers I have selected for the spring designs have either real stories or folk legends somewhere in their history, but none can be more bizarre than that of the tulip. It began in 1544 when the Austrian Ambassador to Turkey, Ogier Ghislain de Busbeca, saw some wild tulips growing near Constantinople and sent a few of the bulbs home to Vienna. These were planted in the Emperor's garden. Later, shipments of bulbs were sold and grown in the gardens of rich Austrian merchants. By 1577 the first tulips arrived in Britain and some years later France enjoyed them too. These tulips were plain ones – red, white, yellow or purple – nothing much to get excited about. All was quiet on the tulip front for almost fifty years, but then a craze for tulips emerged that was to be called 'tulip mania'. Holland was the centre of this extraordinary phenomenon. Suddenly, in 1634, the price of tulips rocketed – an especially prized bulb could cost the price of a house or a farm. Dutch people from every walk of life bought,

sold and speculated in tulip bulbs. It had nothing to do with gardening or even of owning one but was simply a way of making money as is done on the stock market today. People exchanged 'Tulip Notes' which promised to supply a stated number of bulbs. Paper millionaires were created overnight. The Dutch government finally put a stop to this fun by declaring that all the precious 'Tulip Notes' had to be honoured. Overnight the market crashed. The tulip returned to its home in the garden. Today Holland exports over 100 million bulbs around the world at a price that anyone who gardens can afford.

Once winter is past the garden becomes a feast for the eye and the nose which begins with the first crocuses and aconites and goes on to produce blooms until the garden is dense with colour. I hope my selection includes some of the spring flowers you like best.

Many watercolours like this one of Tulips, by the American artist James Hall Hopkins, easily translate into unusual and colourful needlepoint patterns.

PINK MAY

The small design of apple blossom makes a good central pattern for a cushion.

The May or hawthorn hedges of England were once thought to be the meeting places of fairies where witches bounded about gathering the leaves and twigs for their magical qualities. So powerful is folk belief that even today it is difficult to walk along a hedgerow with friends and not be stopped by at least one of them from picking May blossom, with the warning that it will bring bad luck

Yet in other countries hawthorn is considered to bring luck, especially at weddings; and at one time Germans used the branches in funeral pyres so that the soul of the deceased might spring directly up to heaven. In England hawthorn was elevated to high rank when Richard III was slain at Bosworth and his crown was hidden in a hawthorn tree. When it was found and carried by Lord Stanley to make Henry VII the new king of England, a crown in a bush of fruited hawthorn was adopted as a device of the House of Tudor.

The month of April to May is a time of festival, a time to welcome another spring. One way or another most countries in the West seem to have a 'May Day'. It may now be predominantly political in nature, but nevertheless it remains a time when ordinary people celebrate the passing of winter and are joyous at the season of rebirth. In the last century, on May Day morning village youths would meet, usually at a place named the 'May Bank'. Wild flowers were gathered and scattered in a ceremony of thanks around a Maypole.

As round as an apple,
As deep as a cup,
And all the king's horses
Cannot pull it up.
Answer: a well.
A seventeenth-century riddle

In the county of Oxfordshire, local folk would fetch a number of small hawthorn trees to position in front of their homes to ensure that spring stayed.

There are over 3,000 named varieties of apple and each fruit will have begun its life by offering us the spectacle of its bloom. Individual apple flowers seem to have little scent, but in mass they become sweet and delicate, strongest in the early morning in clouds of pale pink and white. In spring the orchards of England are adrift with beauty, and this dignified and simple tree with its annual harvest is so bountiful that most people have apples enough to give away.

COLOURWAYS FOR PINK MAY

FLOWERS   Reds: A941, A943, A866, A504 (PA945, PA947, PA850, PA950)
LEAVES   Greens: A404, A401 (PA605, PA602)   Blues: A522, A154 (PA534, PA524)
BACKGROUND   Yellow: A996 (PA762)

COLOURWAYS FOR APPLE BLOSSOM

FLOWERS   Reds: A621, A622, A942 (PA835, PA834, PA946)   Yellow: A472 (PA726)   Brown: A302 (PA403)   Green: A407 (PA601)
LEAVES   Greens: A407, A404, A402 (PA601, PA602, PA605)

VIOLETS

In Clare, Suffolk, near the old railway station, you can cross a bridge and follow a path grown wild with weeds to a door set in a stone wall. When you open it, you step into the peace of Clare Priory, first home of the Augustinian monks in England. Spread before you in this secret garden lies a spring coverlet of white violets. This modest flower, symbol of humility and herb of sleep, haunts the spring air with its unforgettable fragrance. It is not possible to walk further until you have lingered to admire, to catch the scent, and to reflect on the magical power of coming upon such unexpected beauty.

I know a bank whereon the wild-thyme blows,
Where oxlips and the nodding violet grows;
Quite over-canopied with luscious woodbine,
With sweet musk-roses, and with eglantine:
    'A Midsummer Night's Dream',
    William Shakespeare,
    1564-1616

The first strong scent of violets fades as we smell them so that we think it has vanished, but it is our sense of smell that has been overpowered. For this reason, the scent of violets is always fleeting, as Shakespeare noted:

Sweet, not lasting
The perfume and suppliance of a minute.

There are white, purple and blue violets and it is hard to find someone who dislikes them. Napoleon kept a bunch on his desk. They were the favourite flowers of Elizabeth I. Poets sing of them. In myth, Orpheus fell asleep on the mossy bank of a river and, where he lay, violets first grew. The Victorians had an absolute passion for these flowers too. The violet has long been a symbol of humility so, by wearing the flowers fresh or reproduced in jewellery, Victorian ladies encouraged belief in their womanly modesty and the affectation of shyness and personal reserve so typical of that mannered society.

The rose and the violet are constant companions in one of the most familiar of folk rhymes,

whose opening words are 'Roses are red and violets blue . . .' In England in 1784 you might have heard this one:

The rose is red, the violet's blue,
The honey's sweet, and so are you.

In the *New Yorker* magazine of 13 November 1937, recording sidewalk rhymes of New York children, an entirely different sentiment was expressed on the old theme:

Roses are red, violets are blue,
    I like pecans,
        Nuts to you.

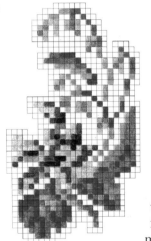

Violets are a fleeting pleasure and I wouldn't pick wild ones and deprive others, so I grow them in my garden. They scatter seeds and spring up in unlikely places where they are left to get on with their own lives. This large design for an embroidered bouquet lets you have violets all the year round. These will not fade and in the winter will be a happy reminder of the first days of spring. I have centred the bouquet within a rectangular frame of flowers. You might wish to make the frame square (see cover).

COLOURWAYS FOR VIOLETS
FLOWERS   Purples: A885, A102, A105, A106 (PA313, PA332, PA570, PA310)   Yellows: A843, A472 (PA702, PA703)   Browns: A764, A762 (PA406, PA405)
LEAVES   Greens: A401, A402, A404, A407 (PA695, PA694, PA692, PA690)   Purple: A106 (PA310)
BORDER FLOWERS   Purples: A885, A102, A105, A106 (PA313, PA332, PA570, PA310)   Yellow: A472 (PA703)   Brown: A762 (PA405)
BORDER LEAVES   Greens: A401, A402, A404 (PA695, PA694, PA692)

COLOURWAYS FOR VIOLET MOTIF
FLOWERS   Purples: A885, A102, A105, A106 (PA313, PA332, PA570, PA310)   Yellows: A472, A843 (PA703, PA702)   Reds: A622, A623, A626 (PA835, PA833, PA830)
LEAVES   Greens: A401, A402, A404 (PA695, PA694, PA692)

TRELLIS AND YELLOW CROCUS

A trellis-work design as the predominant pattern, the background, or as an integral part of the pattern, as in this one for yellow crocus, always makes an attractive finished work. The crocuses here are highly stylized. The single flower repeat can be used without the trellis effect and the border pattern can be worked separately for some other piece in different colours. Trellis work of various kinds is coming back into fashion.

All Nature seems at work. Slugs leave their lair –
The bees are stirring – birds are on the wing –
And Winter, slumbering in the open air,
Wears on his smiling face a dream of Spring!
Samuel Taylor Coleridge, 1772-1834

The use of elaborate corner designs in needlepoint, such as this Entwined Corner Pattern, was a device much favoured by the Victorians.

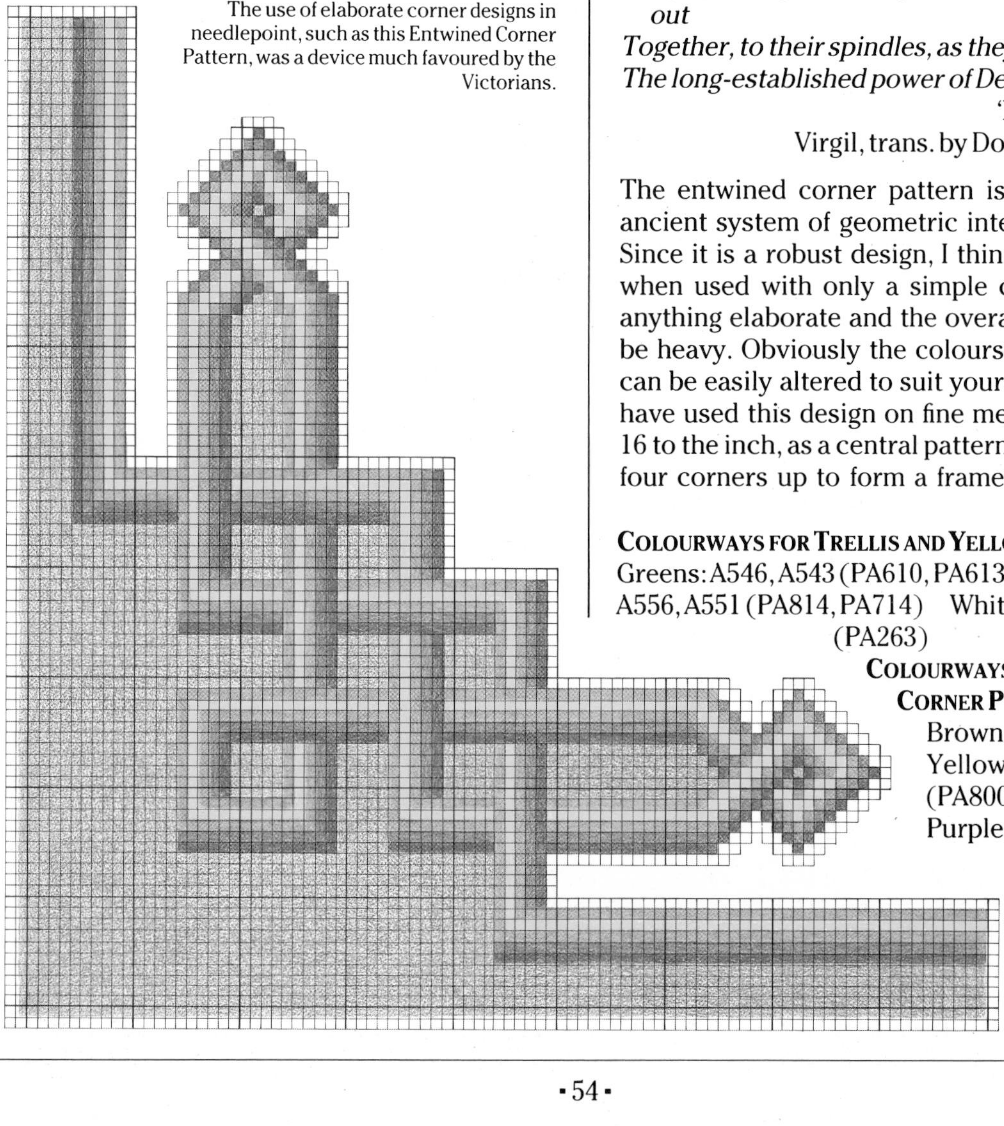

Trellises are pretty and practical as screens and, on their own, make attractive 'sculpture' effects in the garden. In England today trellis work is rather simple, usually being in diamonds or squares, but America offers many more patterns which may be French, Spanish or Chinese in style. The more ornate the trellis, the more carefully it needs to be sited. Its life can be greatly extended if it is framed in solid wood, strong enough to sustain the vigour of climbing plants, and not too lightweight in construction, so that wind and rain do not destroy it in a year or two. I think diamond pattern trellis looks most effective when painted white and set against a red brick wall.

'Keep spinning, circle of years,' the Fates cried
out
Together, to their spindles, as they sang
The long-established power of Destiny.
'Roman Poetry',
Virgil, trans. by Dorothea Wender

The entwined corner pattern is based on the ancient system of geometric interlocking lines. Since it is a robust design, I think it works best when used with only a simple central motif – anything elaborate and the overall effect would be heavy. Obviously the colours I have chosen can be easily altered to suit your own scheme. I have used this design on fine mesh canvas, say 16 to the inch, as a central pattern, by joining the four corners up to form a frame.

COLOURWAYS FOR TRELLIS AND YELLOW CROCUS
Greens: A546, A543 (PA610, PA613)   Yellows:
A556, A551 (PA814, PA714)   White: A992
(PA263)

COLOURWAYS FOR ENTWINED
CORNER PATTERN
Brown: A905 (PA440)
Yellows: A477, A552
(PA800, PA773)
Purple: A102 (PA313)

CLOVER

Beyond the iris walk in my garden is a small pasture. When the clover begins to cover the ground with its green velvet, I know spring is likely to stay warm. There are many different kinds of clover and before the flowers bloom it is hard to tell them apart, although grazing animals have preferences. My goats eat it until the new grass comes up, then they ignore the clover.

April showers bring forth May flowers.

Old Saying

Charles Lamb (1775-1834) wrote to C. C. Clark in December 1828: 'You are knee-deep in clover.' This expression hardly ever means what it says, unless you are a goat! It infers that the person is knee-deep in good luck.

Clover grass is reputed to feel rough to the touch when a storm is brewing. In Norfolk a sprig of clover with only two leaves is used as a charm to ascertain the name of one's future husband. You say to the clover:

A clover, a clover of two,
Put it on your right shoe;
The first young man you
* meet,*
In field, street, or lane,
You'll have him, or one of
* his name.*

Clover Repeat

have to find lucky clover – simply to dream of seeing a field of clover is believed to bring health, prosperity and happiness to lovers.

As clover always seems to grow in clumps whether on the lawn or out in the pasture, I decided to mass the individual leaf for a design. Since I grow two kinds of clover, I drew two different leaves, each in a different colour. There is so much green in the garden itself by late spring that I decided blue, yellow and red would be the colours for my needlepoint clover. When you come to doing the pattern, you may decide that the clover you like best is natural pink and green, or even lavender and pale brown. As with any of these designs, the colours used are entirely your own choice.

The small design which I call Clover Repeat is a geometric interpretation of the leaf and blossom. This repeat can be used over a large area, on its own or as individual squares. You could also link them to form a border. Both the large and small patterns are strong ones and demand attention. If you use either of these as a border, I would make the central design equally bold in order that no one element dominates.

The rarity of a four-leafed clover would account for much of our endowing it with special good fortune. Folklore has it that the four-leafed kind grow only in places frequented by fairies. If you find such a clover, you are supposed to be able to see these fabled creatures.

But what is there about a clover that has produced such strong superstition that we still use it as a charm today? With its three leaves it is symbolic of the Holy Trinity, that powerful central belief of Christianity. It is said that St Patrick used a clover as an example of the Trinity when he converted Ireland, and thus clover became the emblem of that country. You do not even

For a detoxifying herbal tonic mix together 2 cups of clover blossoms, 2 sticks of cinnamon and a heaped teaspoon of grated, dried orange peel. To make the tea, add boiling water to two teaspoons of the mixture and allow it to steep.

COLOURWAYS FOR CLOVER
Blue: A464 (PA542)   Yellow: A844 (PA702)   Red: A504 (PA840)   White: A992 (PA263)
COLOURWAYS FOR CLOVER MOTIF
Blue: A464 (PA542)   Yellow: A844 (PA702) Red: A504 (PA840)   White: A992 (PA263)

FANCY PANSIES AS THEY ARE

Who can resist the pansy with her velvet face? Her name comes from the French *pensée*, a 'thought', and she has long been seen as a symbol of loving remembrance. In Shakespeare's day the flower also went by the name of 'love-in-idleness' and Americans once called them 'Johnny-jump-ups'. This seems very apt when you notice how pansies appear high above their foliage in unexpected places in the garden.

The pansies in this large design are modern ones derived from the show or 'fancy' ones that had been developed in England by the 1840s. They may be bi-coloured or self-coloured. The flowers should be circular, with smooth petals lying flat and evenly over one another, and the face of each has a small yellow eye. Earlier varieties which would have been embroidered in the seventeenth century were simple flowers, more closely resembling the little viola.

COLOURWAYS FOR FANCY PANSIES

FLOWERS   Yellows: A872, A551, A844, A552, A471, A474, A842, A997, A996, A473, A475, A556 (PA714, PA755, PA702, PA773, PA704, PA711, PA726, PA760, PA700, PA764, PA814)   Reds: A864, A862, A947, A226, A145, A149, A994, A756, A759 (PA852, PA854, PA930, PA940, PA922, PA920, PA861, PA903, PA900)   Browns: A311, A184, A187, A915, A126, A127 (PA743, PA433, PA430, PA410, PA481, PA480)   Greens: A544, A997 (PA612, PA760)   Purples: A935, A934, A885, A932 (PA320, PA324, PA322)

BORDER   Greens: A548, A544 (PA610, PA612)   Purple: A884 (PA304)

COLOURWAYS FOR PULMONARIA AND PRIMROSES

YELLOW FLOWERS   Yellows: A551, A553 (PA714, PA712)   Green: A543 (PA613)

PINK FLOWERS   Red: A942 (PA946)   Purple: A104 (PA311)

PURPLE FLOWERS   Purples: A102, A104 (PA313, PA311)   Red: A942 (PA946)

LEAVES AND STEMS   Yellow: A881 (PA263)   Greens: A253, A543, A545 (PA693, PA613, PA611)

BUDS   Blue: A745 (PA503)   Purple: A102 (PA313)

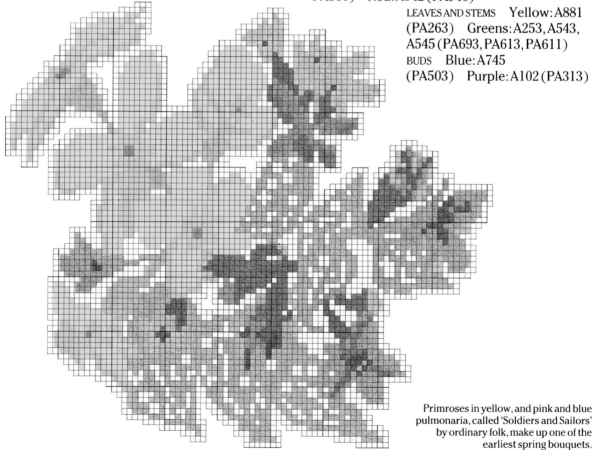

Primroses in yellow, and pink and blue pulmonaria, called 'Soldiers and Sailors' by ordinary folk, make up one of the earliest spring bouquets.

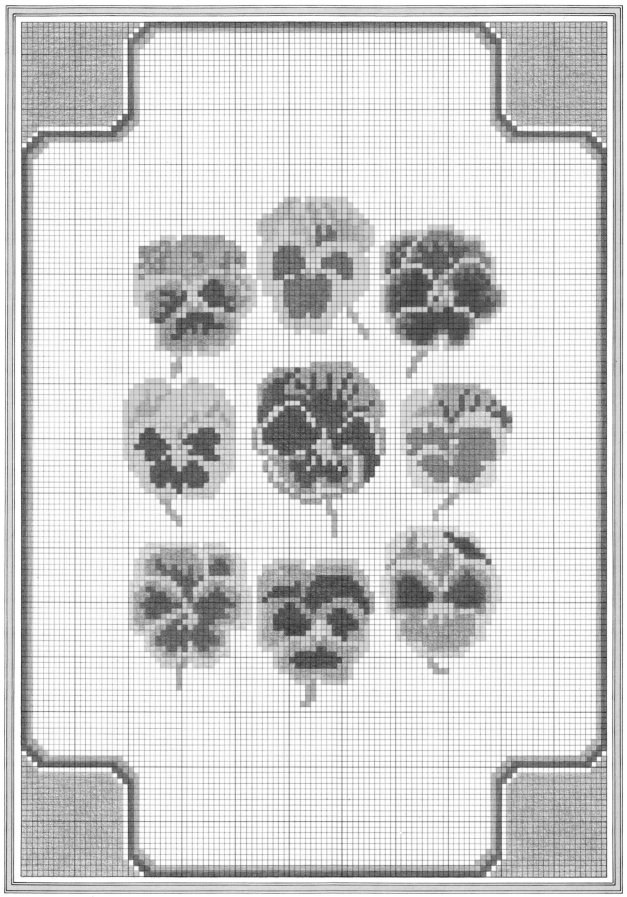

BUMBLE BEE AND LADYBIRD

April seemed only an extension of winter until I spotted the first bumble bee in my garden. He made his way slowly up and down, unsure whether the little warmth in the air had come to stay. The garden had so little to offer him that I felt compelled to design a hot, colourful scene in which he could happily buzz about. Then a ladybird woke up and walked across the curtain, and she too got into the design. It doesn't really qualify for spring, but the three of us enjoyed the false promise of that suddenly warm afternoon while it lasted. It is a complex and 'busy' design in which individual shapes merge. If it looks too bewildering a challenge, then take just one flower sprig for your bumble bee.

COLOURWAYS FOR BUMBLE BEE AND LADYBIRD

BUMBLE BEE   Black: A993 (PA220)   Yellows: A551, A476 (PA714, PA710)

LADYBIRD   Red: A995 (PA941)   Yellow: A551 (PA714)   Black: A993 (PA220)   FLOWERS   Reds: A995, A994, A622 (PA941, PA861, PA941) Yellows: A551, A553 (PA714, PA712)   LEAVES Greens: A253, A404, A407 (PA693, PA602, PA600)

COLOURWAYS FOR POT OF PRIMULAS

POT   Browns: A761, A765, A767 (PA475, PA402, PA400)   FLOWERS   Reds: A504, A995, A505 (PA941, PA950, PA840)   Purple: A149 (PA920) Yellows: A552, A844 (PA713, PA726)   Green: A253 (PA693)   LEAVES   Greens: A256, A253, A251A (PA696, PA693, PA695)

A Pot of Primulas, bright and cheerful, lasts for several weeks and then can be planted out.

CROCUSES

The crocus family contains more than 70 species, and varieties flower between August and April. These dwarf plants are remarkably hardy and, after a long hard winter, it is a surprise to see their fragile flowers sticking up through the cold ground. The flowers do not survive long after picking and, in any case, they are too good an invitation to venture outdoors again for them to be cut and taken back to the house. The range of colours is fairly broad, but mainly they are yellow, orange, white, cream, purple, lavender and bronze, with yellow stamens.

*Day by day the narcissus blooms
in early clusters, fed by the dew
of the sky, from long ago a crown
for the great goddesses, and with it
the gold-lit Crocus.*
     'The Grove of Colonus', Sophocles

The crocus was one of the flowers from which the gods Juno and Jupiter made their bed, so it was often used by the Romans to adorn a nuptial bed. They also made special perfumes from the flowers which were sprinkled over guests at feasts and celebrations.

The colours in these designs work well for decorative objects in a bedroom where the overall decor is pale and feminine. In the large design I have used the device of a silhouette flower in green on a pale green background. Backgrounds like this can be seen in many Victorian canvas embroideries.

After we have enjoyed the spring crocuses we can see them again in the autumn when other varieties bloom. One of these, *Crocus sativus*, is among the oldest of all cultivated plants for it produces saffron, probably the most expensive spice in the world. Used in Spanish, Italian, French and Indian cooking, its name comes from an Arabic word 'Sahafarn' meaning 'thread', for the part of the flower that is used to make bright yellow saffron is the

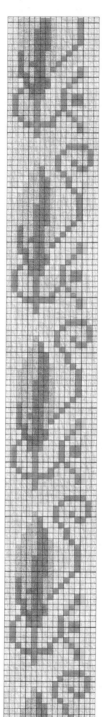

thread-like stigma. In the Middle Ages this versatile spice was used medicinally for measles, depression and jaundice, and to dye cloth and hair. It was also used as a substitute for gold leaf in illuminated manuscripts and in some church vestment embroideries.

It is said that Sir Thomas Smith, Secretary of State to Edward II, introduced the plant to the English village of Walden to bring some industry to the place. It must be a rare example in history when a politician's idea of economics actually worked, for the area became a centre of considerable wealth and eventually changed its name to Saffron Walden.

It takes some 4,000 blooms to produce an ounce of saffron, so the next time you buy a little envelope of the spice do not complain at the price but think of all those flowers and the hours of cultivation, gathering and preparation that someone somewhere in this world did just for you.

Not all that is named saffron is good for you. There lurks in the fields a meadow saffron, *Colchicum autumnale*. If the bulb or corm of this plant is eaten, death can follow from respiratory failure. It was supposedly included by Medea in her sorceress' brews. For those who love gathering food from the wild, in this case I should admire the gentle spring and autumn garden crocus and stick to buying the spice from the supermarket.

COLOURWAYS FOR CROCUSES
FLOWERS   Purples: A884, A885 (PA334, PA332)   Blue: A883
(PA246)   Yellows: A841, A842, A843, A474 (PA715, PA726, PA702, PA710)
FLOWER MOTIF AND BACKGROUND   Greens: A421, A423 (PA624, PA622)
COLOURWAYS FOR CROCUS BORDER
Green: A423 (PA622)   Yellows: A474, A842 (PA710, PA726)   Purples: A884, A885 (PA334, PA332)

DAFFODILS AND JASMINE

This is the first bouquet I pick from my garden in spring. It is a happy one of bright warm yellows, fresh green leaves, upright daffodils, sweet jasmine and curious corylopsis. This last plant is a hardy flowering shrub, native to China and Japan. It flowers very early in the year, producing fragrant bell-shaped flowers in drooping racemes of pale yellow or yellow-green. Some varieties can grow to ten feet and the plant does well in ordinary garden soil which is almost lime-free. Corylopsis is well worth garden space for such early spring colour. The bouquet is designed so that you can work the top half of it if you want a smaller pattern.

The name for jasmine is from the Arabic in which the first part of the word meant 'despair' and the second 'illusion', to remind us that to despair is a mistake. The winter-flowering jasmine, *Jasminum nudiflorum* in my design, is a late arrival to the English cottage garden. It can be easily trained up a trellis or against a wall, although it will need some pinning.

I once had a garden in which there was a long forgotten village pond which had been filled in. The water still rose in winter and under the spring grass left a damp bed – just right for that shy plant, *Fritillaria meleagris*, which can prove reluctant to grow where you put it. From drawings and paintings one imagines that it is very tiny but in my garden the plants grew well above the height of the wild grass.

The name Fritillaria comes from the Latin *Fritillus*, meaning a dice box which opens out into a games board with a chequer pattern. This pattern is the same as the flower petals of the plant and this feature is a rarity in nature, for few other plants, if any, boast a perfectly geometric pattern of squares.

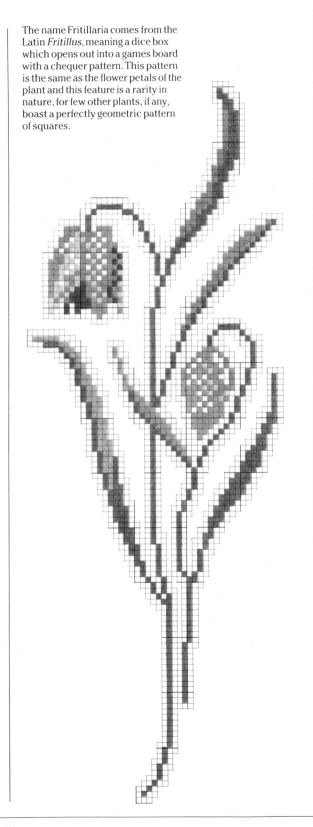

COLOURWAYS FOR DAFFODILS AND JASMINE

DAFFODILS Yellows: A551, A553, A842, A555 (PA714, PA712, PA726, PA770) Brown: A761 (PA474) Greens: A356, A251A (PA603, PA695) Red: A861 (PA858)

JASMINE Yellow: A844 (PA726) Green: A831 (PA662)

CORYLOPSIS Greens: A253, A402 (PA641, PA693) Brown: A913 (PA471)

LEAVES AND STEMS Greens: A831, A356, A253, A402 (PA662, PA603, PA641, PA693) Brown: A913 (PA471)

COLOURWAYS FOR FRITILLARIA

FLOWERS Purples: A104, A102, A884, A883 (PA312, PA314, PA325, PA246)

LEAVES AND STEMS Greens: A353, A354 (PA314, PA312)

PIGEON ON A GATE

Not all the things in the garden are plants, and, friend or foe, the pigeon is a likely visitor to a town or country garden. If you have a wrought-iron gate or fence, he may be seen there surveying the scene and cooing to his spouse, just as in this design which I have done for pure fun. Fancy ironwork as well as wooden trellis-work does, however, lend itself to needlepoint. Do the pigeon or the gate separately if you like. The bird in my picture is the collared dove which has spread throughout Europe in the last seventy years, having arrived from India. This bird is like the house sparrow; it prefers human company and will therefore sit in your garden trees. It will also eat all the buds and berries given a chance. All this seems a far cry from the dove as a symbol of peace. When Noah sent it out to see if the waters had abated, the dove brought back an olive branch to show that the waters had receded and that God had made peace with man.

In France the pigeon hardly ever escapes the wrath of farmers or the cook's pot. At least in France, pigeons are no longer considered a means of curing health complaints. There was a time when the bird was cut open and applied hot to the head of a patient. This messy treatment was supposed to cure both madness and pleurisy. In England the pigeon fared better from the medical men – it was only used as a last resort since there was a taboo against a person dying while lying on a bed of pigeon feathers. When the English used the pigeon for cures, they went to the other end of the body to apply it, as Samuel Pepys recorded when he was urgently called to visit a dear friend who was near to death: 'his breath rattled in his throat and they did lay pigeons at his feet and all despair of him.'

Wrought ironwork lends itself to needlepoint.

Pie made from pigeon is traditional farm fare.

PIGEON PIE

2-3 woodpigeon; stock or water; 1 large onion, chopped; 8 oz (225 g) sliced mushrooms; 2 oz (50 g) butter; 1 tablespoon flour; 6 rashers bacon; 3 hard-boiled eggs; salt, pepper and parsley; bouquet garni; 8 oz (225 g) puff or shortcrust pastry; 1 egg for glazing.

Put the birds in a pan. Add the bouquet garni, salt and pepper. Cover with stock. Simmer, covered, until the meat begins to part from the bone. Drain the birds and cut away the meat from the bones in good-sized pieces. Next, brown the onions and mushrooms in the butter. Stir in the flour and enough stock to make a fairly thick sauce. Let this simmer. Cut up the bacon into pieces to make small rolls and lightly grill. Arrange them around the meat along with quarters of hard-boiled egg. Add salt, pepper and chopped parsley. Pour on the sauce. Cover with pastry and brush over with beaten egg. Bake for 30 minutes at 210°C/425°F/Gas 7, lowering the heat once the pastry has risen well and begins to brown.

COLOURWAYS FOR PIGEON ON A GATE

PIGEON   Greys: A961, A963 (PA204, PA203)   Black: A993 (PA220)   White: A991 (PA262)

Blue: A747 (PA501)   Reds: A503, A721, A725 (PA951, PA862, PA860)

Yellow: A552 (PA773)   Browns: A761, A903 (PA474, PA442)

GATE   Blues: A742, A821, A747 (PA505, PA544, PA501)   Black: A993 (PA220)

COLOURWAYS FOR WROUGHT IRON MOTIF

Blues: A852, A742, A821, A747 (PA500, PA505, PA554, PA501)   Blacks: A875, A961, A963 (PA213, PA204, PA203)   Browns: A761, A903, A905 (PA474, PA442, PA440)

TULIPS AND SPRING FLOWERS

There is a certain luxury in having a big vase of tulips in the house. I suppose this feeling arises from the fact that tulips are so singular and, because the spring garden needs to boast of every flower, to pick a bouquet seems a great extravagance.

See how the flowers, as at parade,
Under their colours stand display'd;
Each regiment in order grows,
That of the tulip, pink, and rose.
But when the vigilant patrol
Of stars walks round about the pole,
Their leaves, that to the stalks are curl'd,
Seem to their staves the ensigns furl'd.
Then in some flower's belovèd hut,
Each bee, as sentinel, is shut,
And sleeps so too; but if once stirr'd,
She runs you through, nor asks the word.
          'Upon Appleton House: To My Lord Fairfax',
                    Andrew Marvell, 1621-1678

There are so many types of tulips that the Royal Horticultural Society and the Dutch Bulb Growers Association undertook to classify all the known ones. They needed *fifteen divisions* to fit in the hundreds of known tulips.

One division is so remarkable that it is named 'Rembrandt'. The tulips shown in the large design are early red ones called 'Brilliant Star' which open out to expose their dark centres. Once picked, a vase of tulips changes shape, rearranging itself as the flowers open and finally twisting straight stems into rococo curves, the flowers flopping open and curling back their petals.

COLOURWAYS FOR TULIPS
TULIPS   Reds: A505, A502, A945, A995 (PA941, PA971, PA953, PA840)   Yellow: A553 (PA772)   Black: A993 (PA220)
LEAVES AND STEMS   Greens: A545, A548 (PA611, PA661)
BORDER   Red: A502 (PA971)
COLOURWAYS FOR SPRING FLOWERS
FLOWERS   Reds: A622, A623 (PA835, PA833)   Yellow: A551 (PA714)   White: A991B (PA260)
LEAVES   Greens: A427, A423, A421 (PA696, PA623, PA624)

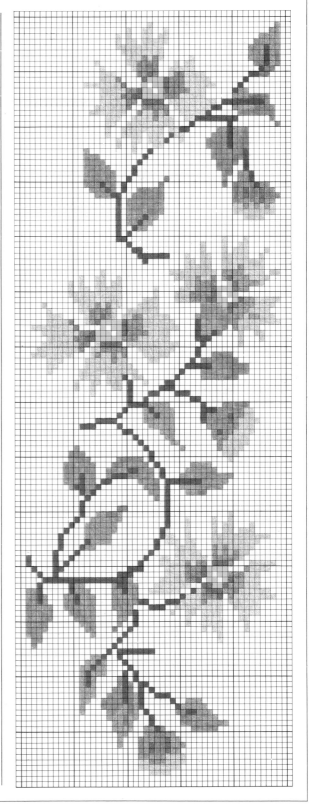

FORGET-ME-NOTS

How the forget-me-not got its name is in some question. It was taken by Henry IV of England as a personal emblem in the belief that whoever wore it would not be forgotten. This means the flower then must have been widely considered to signify remembrance. But the name seems to have gained real popularity when the poet Coleridge in 1817 wrote a poem, 'The Keepsake', in which he called them forget-me-nots. The key lines are as follows:

Nor can I find, amid my lonely walk
By rivulet, or spring, or wet roadside
That blue and bright-eyed floweret of the brook,
Hope's gentle gem, the sweet Forget-me-not!

The idea that the forget-me-not meant love and remembrance probably spread to England from Germany, Denmark, Sweden and France, where it is still sold growing in pots in the flower markets in spring.

The individual forget-me-not is among the most dainty flowers in the garden. This large design repeating a number of the flowers is based on how they appear growing in clumps where seed has blown them. I think they appear at their best when they plant themselves this way. You can extend the pattern in any direction. Even the botanical name of this flower, *Myosotis*, is endearing for it means 'mouse-ear'.

Spring sighed, and through the driving gale
Her warm breath caught the falling snow,
And from the flakes a flower as pale
Did into spotless whiteness blow;
Hope smiling saw the blossom fall,
And watched its root strike in the earth –
'I will that flower the snowdrop call,'
Said Hope, 'In memory of its birth;
And through all ages it shall be
In reverence held, for love of me.'
   'The Snowdrop', Thomas Miller, 1807-1874

The snowdrop is the fair maiden of February. It was grown during the Middle Ages in monasteries and used in the ritual of the purification of the Virgin Mary which was held on 2nd February. When the statue of Mary was temporarily removed for the ceremony, snowdrops were put in the empty place. In the snowdrop design you will need to use a fairly strong background colour in order for the white flowers to show up. You could also use a darker shade of wool to give a stronger outline to the petals of the flowers.

COLOURWAYS FOR FORGET-ME-NOTS
FLOWERS   Blues: A461, A462, A464, A746, A823 (PA546, PA545, PA543, PA502, PA551)   Yellow: A844 (PA726)
BORDER   Blues: A461, A462, A464 (PA546, PA545, PA543)   Yellow: A844 (PA726)   Green: A252 (PA694)

COLOURWAYS FOR SNOWDROPS
FLOWERS   White: A992 (PA261)   Black: A886 (PA564)   Greens: A253, A423 (PA693, PA622)
LEAVES AND STEMS   Greens: A421, A423, A425, A253 (PA623, PA622, PA698, PA693)
BACKGROUND   Blue: A744 (PA504)
BORDER   Green: A425 (PA698)

A LADY'S BOUQUET

At long last a real bouquet of mixed flowers from the garden with the knowledge that there will be many more as spring rolls into summer with its glorious abundance of blooms and, not to be forgotten, its demand for weeding and watering.

This bouquet is in the tradition of both Victorian bouquets and Berlin Artwork patterns. It contains several flowers that would hardly ever have been forgotten whether they were real or embroidered ones – the rose and the pansy, with a satin ribbon to tie them together.

The Victorians inherited a folk tradition based on religious symbolism that was called 'the language of flowers'. Each flower stood for a word or sentiment so that a flower or bouquet could be sent as a message to someone. It is a charming conceit. The language of flowers as a floral code really took off in 1718 when Lady Mary Wortley Montagu sent home a letter to England from Constantinople. She described how the Turkish people used flowers to send messages – a young man knew that if his beloved sent an iris it meant 'no' but if she sent a grape hyacinth it meant 'yes'. Lady Mary's letter was later published and this concept of a language of flowers became popular in England.

By the nineteenth century the idea of sending secret messages became widely fashionable. Young women memorized the floral code. The recipient of the flowers had merely to touch her lips to them to say 'yes' or tear off a petal from one to say 'no'. What each flower signified became complex and often confusing which must have made for much laughter and, in a few cases, tears. Not knowing which flower meant what could lead to a real blunder. For example, an amaryllis meant 'Beautiful though you undoubtedly are, you leave my heart cold,' and belladonna got right to the point, 'I don't trust you, you are too catty.' Most girls possessed a romantic little volume full of pretty pictures and rather awful verse which told them the meaning of each flower. This was a treasured possession in the days when the minuet of courtship was full of flirtations and, apparently, carefully selected nosegays. After the First World War, greater personal freedom and fewer social formalities meant that the language of flowers had little place in modern living.

Here is a short list of flower language. What are the flowers saying in my design for a Lady's Bouquet composed of forget-me-nots, poppies, a rose and pansies?

Anemone	Forsaken
Bluebell	Constancy
Buttercup	Ingratitude
Carnation	Marriage
Cyclamen	Heart
Daisy	Adoration
Forget-me-not	Remember
Foxglove	Insincerity
Geranium	Preference
Heather	Solitude
Iris	Sorrow
Jasmine	Grace
Lilac	First Love
Lily of the Valley	Sweetness
Lupin	Hurt
Marigold	Grief
Mignonette	Gentleness
Narcissus	Coldness
Nasturtium	Patriotism
Orange blossom	Chastity
Pansy	Friend
Poppy	True
Rose	Love
Snapdragon	Revenge
Stock	Beauty
Snowdrop	Purity
Tulip	I love you
Violet	Humility

COLOURWAYS FOR A LADY'S BOUQUET

POPPIES   Reds: A626, A623, A441 (PA831, PA833, PA820)   Yellows: A551, A554 (PA771, PA801)
FORGET-ME-NOTS   Blues: A464, A462, A465 (PA542, PA545, PA540)   Yellows: A844, A696, A694 (PA844, PA751, PA753)
PANSIES   Purples: A106, A105, A103, A102, A101 (PA570, PA310, PA312, PA313, PA314)   Yellows: A694, A696, A551 (PA753, PA751, PA714)   Brown: A581 (PA460)
ROSE   Reds: A941, A943, A945, A948 (PA947, PA945, PA943, PA940)   White: A991 (PA262)
RIBBON   Purples: A106, A105, A103, A101 (PA570, PA310, PA312, PA314)
LEAVES AND STEMS   Greens: A548, A546, A545, A544, A253 (PA660, PA610, PA611, PA612, PA693)

Too quick despairer, wherefore wilt thou go?
Soon will the high Midsummer pomps come on,
Soon will the musk carnations break and swell,
Soon will we have gold-dusted snapdragon,
Sweet-William with its homely cottage smell,
And stocks in fragrant blow,
Roses that down the alleys shine afar,
And open jasmine-muffled lattices,
And groups under the dreaming garden trees,
And the full moon, and the white evening-star.

'Thyrsis', Matthew Arnold, 1822-1888

SUMMER

How right the French writer Colette was when she noted that nothing passes fast in summer except summer itself. In England that can be taken literally in some years, hence the old saying that our summer consists of two sunny days followed by a thunderstorm. While it can rain and rain *and* rain, there are summers in which the weather is perfect. For a little while the English enjoy their gardens without discussing the climate. As we grow older, we look back on the summers of childhood – those romantic days which were envelopes of white light, dappled tree shadows, fields of dandelions, and the taste of ice cream. There were the lonely games that didn't feel lonely at all – picking away the petals of a flower, turning upside-down campanula or columbine to make dancing ladies, condemning butterflies by our touch. Summer was the season we hugged in pure alliance of heart.

In a competition to name the flowers of summer, everyone would probably win, for there are so many of them: tall spires of azure delphiniums, pyramids of lupins, phlox with a dozen little flowers, clove-scented pinks and carnations, wands of saxifrage, soldiers of verbascum, sweet strawberries, handfuls of cherries the birds may have spared us, and, in a rush of colour, the poppies, achilleas, hollyhocks, borage, lavatera, salvia, veronica, snapdragons, stocks and honeysuckle. Finally, no one would forget the fragrant trumpets of the lilies and the roses, symbol of love.

In romance and embroidery the rose has long spoken of love. A bouquet of red roses can hardly mean anything else to a woman, and the pink rosebud tucked away in a bouquet speaks of tenderness and hope. There are many roses, and each kind has a special message for the person who receives one.

ROSE LANGUAGE

A rosebud with leaves and thorns: I hope for love
A rosebud without leaves: Love may be lost
A rosebud without thorns: Love may be gained
Bud of a moss rose: Confessions of love
Bud of a red rose: Pure and lovely
Bud of a white rose: Charm and innocence
An unopened rose: Unawakened love
A rose and two buds: Secrets shared
A full rose: Beauty
Cabbage rose: Grace
Musk rose: Charm
Single rose: Simplicity
Damask rose: Bashful love
Dog rose: Pleasure
Eglantine: Poetry
Garland of roses: Virtue and beauty
Moss rose: Voluptuous love
Pink rose: Our love is perfect happiness
Red and white roses: Unity
Rosa Mundi: Variety
Thornless rose: Early attachment
Faded rose: Beauty is fleeting
Miniature Roses: Gentleness
White rose: Dreams

There was no question about including roses and most of the other favourites in the designs

The grass-leaved flag.

for summer, but some were left out in favour of flowers like nasturtiums, sunflowers, and geraniums that are in so many ordinary gardens in England and, with little attention, repay us with vivid colour.

In addition to these flowers, designs for summer include a pattern for little scattered flowers with a Victorian fancy border; flower motifs which can be repeated and are very suitable for needlepoint destined for upholstering a chair; a geometric pattern incorporating a rose set in blocks of colour; and a huge bouquet typical of the Berlin Artwork patterns of the last century. Looking around my garden, there were quite a few visitors, and some of these are in this season's designs: a rabbit in a strawberry patch; bees busy making honey; and a bird stealing a cherry. Last but not least, my adored cat, king of every leaf of catmint.

The colours of the summer garden, like beauty itself, are in the eyes of the beholder. If you don't think my idea of the colour of the roses, lilies or other flowers in the designs is right when you buy your wools, then please make them the colour you see. In this blessed season of the year, nothing is wrong. (Well, perhaps the lemonade does need just a touch more sugar.)

Went to pluck a garden posy;
Passed the lavender and lily;
Passed the pinks and passed the red roses –
Nettles were what made up my posies.
Old Welsh Harp Verse, translated by Glyn Jones

All these dreamy memories of childhood and sitting about sipping lemonade or tea on the lawn, slowly pushing a needle in and out of an embroidery we had promised to finish in time for *last* Christmas, are all very well – but what of the lawn and the weeds? The lawn must be cut, and

in this day of equality and modern machinery that is merely a boring task. As to weeds, let's try to be friends, for in the end they will win. If you do not believe me, just try to free a garden of that monastic survivor, ground elder.

Once upon a time folk gathered and ate the young leaves of this plant in the spring. Once upon a time I also tried eating them, out of rage at their persistence in a bed of iris. Even with masses of butter they tasted like a bitter version of tired spinach. Still, if you are defeated by ground elder, there is bound to be some twitch grass or stinging nettles to keep you on your toes. Can you ever be friends with these plants? Yes, if you treat them like food crops. I don't suggest you harvest ground elder, but dandelion salad is à French treat, or you could make nettle beer or cook chickweed which does, in this case, taste like young spinach.

We forget how useful such 'weeds' really are. For example, nettles can be spun and made into fine cloth like linen, and this was how they were once used from the earliest days of spinning and weaving; the finished fabric is known as 'nettle cloth'. An early Bronze Age grave in Denmark yielded some textile fragments that proved to be woven from common stinging nettle. The way in which the nettle is prepared for spinning demands fresh, running water. The plant is gathered, tied in bundles, and placed in a stream for about three weeks. During this time the green part rots away and is removed by the current. When this has happened, the remainder of the plant is taken out and thoroughly dried. Then, the plant is beaten to get out the fibres, which are spun like flax.

Nettle thread was probably used as a weft thread in weaving rather than for the warp. It is one of the best linen-type threads and was once called 'the poor man's flax', which is rather derogatory, considering that from a weaver's standpoint it is a beautiful thread with which to work and produces fine, strong cloth.

Now as I was young and easy under the apple
*　　boughs*
About the lilting house and happy as the grass
*　　was green,*
*　　The night above the dingle starry,*
*　　　Time let me hail and climb*
*　　Golden in the heydays of his eyes,*
And honoured among wagons I was prince of the
*　　apple towns*
And once below a time I lordly had the trees and
*　　leaves*
*　　　Trail with daisies and barley*
*　　Down the rivers of the windfall light.*

And as I was green and carefree, famous among
*　　the barns*
About the happy yard and singing as the farm
*　　was home,*
*　　In the sun that is young once only,*
*　　　Time let me play and be*
*　　Golden in the mercy of his means,*
And green and golden I was huntsman and
*　　herdsman, the calves*
Sang to my horn, the foxes on the hills barked
*　　clear and cold,*
*　　　And the sabbath rang slowly*
*　　In the pebbles of the holy streams.*
　　　　　　'Fern Hill', Dylan Thomas, 1914-1953

Couch or twitch grass travels the world. You will discover it in your English garden, on the continent, and in America. It advances with little underground stems that give rise to ever more new plants and it is the bane of modern gardeners, who seem constantly to be digging it up and burning it. Yet, this little weed is a rich source of potassium, silica, chlorine and other desirable mineral nutrients and is a plant of importance in herbal medicine. It is likely that your dog or cat when feeling poorly will seek this grass as a remedy. In a word, it is a friend not a foe. So I suggest you stop burning it at the stake, and when you have pulled it up, make a liquid feed of it to nourish your flowers.

　You could also make tea for yourself as the French do. Here is how: to 1 oz (25 g) of cleaned roots cut into short lengths put 1 pint (600 ml) of boiling water. Let this sit with a cover on it. Take this freely by the small wine-glass. It doesn't have much taste and you can flavour it with some lemon or a little honey if you prefer.

June 6th (1768). In the lane at the foot of my garden is a dog-rose now in bloom and very sweet to smell, so I suffer it to grow over my wall and take pleasure to walk by there in the evening. My bees come staggering home from the clover and are like to swarm soon. In the garden they cluster about the broom I planted two years ago, and many insects hang about the honeysuckle as if it were a tavern. It is the sweet stillness of the long light evenings which do hold me most, being as much like to prayer as may be, though Lord knows I am a sinful man enough yet soothed by garden peace which, of itself, is good. The swifts cease their joyous screaming as the dusk falls, yet one or two will still fly high, then skim the earth as if they looked for lost playmates.
A Diary of an Eighteenth-Century Garden,
J. R. Anderson

CHERRIES

Bird with a Cherry.

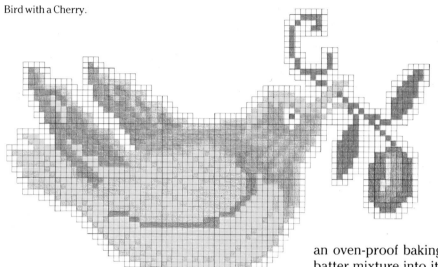

CHERRY FLAN

Preheat oven to 180°C/ 350°F/Gas 4. Remove stones from ¾ lb (350 g) of fresh cherries. Put the following ingredients into a liquidizer in this order: ½ pt (300 ml) milk, 2 oz (50 g) sugar, 3 eggs, 1 tsp vanilla extract, ⅛ tsp salt, 2½ oz (62 g) sifted white flour. Blend this mixture at top speed for at least one minute. Next, butter an oven-proof baking dish. Pour a little of the batter mixture into it and gently warm the dish over moderate heat until the batter just sets. This gives the flan a firm base on which to place the fruit. Spread the cherries over this batter base and sprinkle on about 2 oz (50 g) sugar – less if the cherries are sweet, more if they are a bit acid. Pour on the rest of the batter and put in the oven. It will be done when the sides have lifted slightly away from the dish and the centre no longer looks uncooked. Serve while warm if possible. Don't refrigerate, as this hardens the flan. The cherry, considered in former times to be one of the Fruits of Heaven, can be seen in many embroideries, especially in samplers. The fruit is traditionally held by a bird, as in this design. Cherries were known in Babylon, and it is a pleasant fancy to imagine that cherry trees hung with blossom drifted on the terraces of the Hanging Gardens.

There seems to be a certain ratio between the number of birds that frequent your garden, how much garden food is about for them, and the damage they will do to your cherry crop. Once I had two cherry trees. Each summer I got pounds of the fruit – enough for cherry flans and for making jam in winter. Neighbours were surprised and envious, for the birds had taken their crops. Why not mine? I wondered. The answer, as far as I can see, was that for several years the garden around my cherry trees had been left wild and overgrown. There was a waiting harvest of seeds and strawberries on offer to any passing bird. I think they stopped at my place for a change of diet between raids on the neighbours' cherries.

Cherry-ripe, ripe, ripe I cry,
Full and fair ones; come and buy.
If so be you ask me where
They do grow, I answer: There,
Where my Julia's lips do smile;
There's the land, or cherry-isle,
Whose plantations fully show
All the year where cherries grow.
    'Cherry Ripe', Robert Herrick, 1591-1674

A traditional French peasant dish, Cherry Flan is about the easiest dessert you could ever make. Here is the recipe.

COLOURWAYS FOR CHERRY REPEAT

CHERRIES   Reds: A942, A945, A995 (PA946, PA953, PA941)

LEAVES AND STEMS   Greens: A431, A435 (PA687, PA683)

COLOURWAYS FOR BIRD WITH A CHERRY

BIRD   Browns: A302, A304 (PA403, PA411)   Yellow: A552 (PA773)   Blue: A464 (PA543)   Green: A425 (PA698)   White: A992 (PA262)   Black: A993 (PA220)

CHERRY   Reds: A942, A945, A995 (PA946, PA953, PA941)

LEAVES AND STEM   Green: A435 (PA683)

FLOWERS IN A FIELD

The use of little flowers in repeating pattern remains a favourite of French needlepoint workers, and needlepoint canvas already printed with such flowers comes by the metre in most of their wool shops. The more packed the flowers appear, the more I think the finished work looks like damask. The more delicate and pastel the shading of the flowers, the more they seem to resemble the scattered flowers one sees in woven tapestries, one of the finest examples being *La Dame à la Licorne* (Brussels, *c.* 1480-1490), which can be seen in the Musée de Cluny, Paris. Two other good examples of flowers as background can be seen in the late fifteenth-century French tapestry *Feudal Life, The Bath*, and in the Flemish tapestry *The Triumphs of Petrarch – the Triumph of Time over Fame* in the Kunsthistorisches Museum, Vienna. When you do a background of small flowers therefore, you are following an ancient tradition.

This design for flowers without using the border is a good one for chair seat covers or other upholstery. I have also used it as a background to a larger work in the woven-tapestry tradition. The first time I did them in this way, I embroidered pastel shades on a cream ground. Eventually the flowers merged with the background until you could hardly see one from the other, which was a real waste of time. I learned that the best way was to work the flowers in a sufficiently strong shade to see them – so the shade of the ground colour does not matter. The border in this design can be used to frame any of the patterns for flowers.

The four great flowers of the East have long been the camellia, the chrysanthemum, the azalea and the paeony.

In Roman times, Pliny the Elder called the paeony the oldest of all cultivated flowers. Whether or not this is true no one can say, but certainly the paeony has long been part of the ancient culture of China.

It has survived all manner of changes including the recent Cultural Revolution and remains a feature of Chinese art, literature, and daily life,

Paeony

appearing on such everyday items as postage stamps. The old Empress of China had such a passion for the paeony that she diverted funds from her navy to enlarge her gardens and her paeony collection. Ever yearning for new and more exotic plants, the Victorians also spent much time and money in futile searches for legendary specimens such as the fabled Chinese blue paeony which, as far as is known, does not exist. Unless, of course, the old Empress had one. Meanwhile, we can enjoy pink, red, white, yellow, plain and frilled paeonies in our own gardens. These plants, with their dislike of being disturbed once planted, have an ancient dignity not unlike that of the distinguished oriental civilization which revered them.

COLOURWAYS FOR FLOWERS IN A FIELD
Yellow: A551 (PA714)   Purple: A603
(PA313)   Reds: A943, A947 (PA945, PA940)
BORDER   Greens: A423, A427 (PA623, PA696)
COLOURWAYS FOR PAEONIA
FLOWER   Reds: A943, A948 (PA945, PA940)
LEAVES AND STEM   Greens: A525, A834 (PA522, PA661)

HONEY BEES

A salt papyrus manuscript in the British Museum tells of the ancient Egyptians' belief that the tears of the god Re were turned into bees, thus showing the miraculous power of nature embodied in this most industrious of creatures.

The god Re wept and the tears from his eyes fell on the ground and turned into a bee. The bee made his comb and busied himself with the flowers of every plant; And so wax was made and also honey out of the tears of the god Re.

The belief that bees possess supernatural powers is not confined just to ancient civilizations or our own ancestors. The Egyptian belief is directly echoed in a Breton French one which says that bees sprang from the tears of Christ on the cross, and one German folktale says bees were created to provide candles for the Church – a romantic but all-serves-man attitude to nature. This idea may have been one of the main reasons behind the long-held custom of informing the bees of a death in the family – the 'telling of the bees'. In England someone would hurry from the house in mourning to the bee hives in the garden. Tapping on the front entrance to the hive, they would say:

Bees, bees, awake!
Your master is dead
And another you must take.

Then a little piece of funeral cake would be left for the bees and some black crêpe tied around the hive.

At weddings on the island of Guernsey, wedding streamers were used to decorate hives, and in Leicestershire, the bees got a good deal because part of the wedding cake was left outside the hives for them to eat.

Swarming bees are another matter and mean bad events are about to happen, like a house fire or death in the family. If your bees swarm, the thing to do if you are in Somerset is to rub the hive with mint. If you are in Yorkshire, dip a branch of elder in sugar and water and wave it over the swarm. If that doesn't work, then there is nothing for it but to get out your jam-making pans and beat them in the hope that the noise will control the swarm. These instructions were prescribed once upon a time, but today, of course, you should ring up your local bee keepers' association and ask for someone to take away the swarm.

My son, eat thou honey, because it is good; and the honeycomb, which is sweet to thy taste: so shall the knowledge of wisdom be unto thy soul.
Proverbs, 24, 13-14

Honey to eat for health and to use for beauty continue to be concepts and practices vigorously endorsed by millions of people, including the romantic novelist Barbara Cartland, who attributes her vigorous good health and longevity in no small measure to the benefits of honey. It is delicious as a sweetener and can be used in many recipes. The better the honey, the more likely it is to be expensive. But like all such things, the cost is relative to quality and pleasure. The fragrance and taste of local honey is not to be compared to the bland blended honey found in the average supermarket. Wherever you live, look around for a local beekeeper and buy some of his or her honey. The quality of the local bee brew is always apt to be better.

COLOURWAYS FOR HONEY BEES
BEES   Greens: A354, A353 (PA604, PA602)   Brown: A184 (PA433)   Yellows: A844 or A556 (PA726 or PA814)   Black: A998 (PA221)
FLOWERS AND LEAVES   Blues: A464, A461, A462 (PA542, PA546, PA545)   Black: A998 (PA221)   Yellows: A552, A477, A844 (PA773, PA800, PA702)   Greens: A548, A544, A253 (PA610, PA612, PA693)
COLOURWAYS FOR BEE BORDER
Green: A423 (PA622)   Brown: A184 (PA433)   Yellow: A552 (PA773)

NASTURTIUMS AND POPPIES

The most splendid display of nasturtiums I have ever seen was not in an English garden at all. They were grown by an expatriate Liverpool sailor by the name of Frank Jackson, who has lived for many years on the little Spanish island of Formentera. There he built a house of local stone by himself, and put the garden together over the years by carrying pails of good soil to his new house. He made a long screen of cotton string like a large net along one of his garden paths. It was perhaps thirty feet in length. He grew nasturtiums up this net and they formed a living coverlet of orange, red and yellow throughout the long hot island summer.

Nasturtiums can be added successfully to any design where flowers are wanted and always seem pleasing, trailing themselves about, peeking from clusters of leaves, and rising above the leaves with bright blooms, characteristic 'spurs' and many small buds. Here the large design, with its central motif of a small group of the flowers and leaves, moves outward to use the flower in a more abstract version for the lattice effect. A nasturtium-flower border encloses the design. I worked the central motif only, then machine-sewed ribbon around it as a frame, and made it into a small cushion for a bedroom chair. The central motif, the lattice work and the border may all be used as separate designs.

Poppies

COLOURWAYS FOR NASTURTIUMS
BACKGROUND TRELLIS   Greens: A404, A401 (PA601, PA604)   Red: A441 (PA823)   Yellow: A843 (PA726)   BORDER   Greens: A401, A404 (PA604, PA601)   Reds: A441, A444 (PA823, PA821)
FLOWERS   Reds: A441, A444, A148, A995, A942 (PA823, PA821, PA921, PA941, PA946)   Yellows: A843, A557 (PA726, PA813)   Brown: A915 (PA423)   Green: A253 (PA693)
LEAVES   Greens: A401, A404, A407, A253 (PA604, PA601, PA660, PA693)

COLOURWAYS FOR POPPIES
FLOWER   Reds: A622, A626, A624 (PA833, PA831, PA834)   Black: A993 (PA220)   Yellow: A553 (PA712)   LEAVES AND STEMS   Greens: A251A, A426 (PA694, PA621)

When it comes to poppies in the English garden, I like the big oriental ones, *Papaver orientale*, originally from Armenia. This is a hardy and spreading border plant that forms clumps with flowers up to 4 inches in diameter. The colours are scarlet, pink, carmine, salmon pink, orange, and white, most with a black blotch at the base of the petals. Being some 2 to 3 feet high, they are usually found at the back of the border. I mix mine with blue and purple iris, so they bloom together at more or less the same time. I am left, of course, with a glorious mess of sprawling poppy stems and flopping flowers and iris leaves turning brown in the summer heat. Still, the moment of their blooming is a real treat.

ROSES

If you want to plant a garden with historic as well as old-fashioned roses like these, you might include the Old Cabbage Rose or Provence Rose with its fat flowers of many petals; the White Rose of York, *Rosa alba semi-plena*; the Gallica Rose which in England is called the Apothecary's Rose; Rosa Mundi with its white flowers striped with deep pink and crimson; and the Great Maiden's Blush Rose, once called in France *Cuisse de Nymphe Emue*, the Thigh of the Passionate Nymph.

In my garden I have a Reine des Violettes which bears quartered blooms that especially please me.

The choice is large and glorious, and even if they only bloom once with an occasional later flush, unlike modern floribundas, these old roses are the brief encounter at the beginning of summer that makes you glad to be out in the fresh air.

A single rose centered on a canvas and surrounded by a pretty border makes an attractive cushion. The border might be of small flowers in the dark pink.

Old-fashioned roses have enjoyed a revival in English gardens in the last few years and a number of nurseries now specialize in these types, such is their popularity. These roses, often shrub-like in habit, were widely planted in Tudor times. Robust of habit, they are worth planting if only for their fragrance, for they possess a lush perfume. Sometimes the fragrance is of damask, sometimes of raspberries, cloves or cinnamon. The flowers can be double or globular like paeonies, or small rosettes more bud than bloom. Shakespeare knew many of these old roses, and perhaps it was of the Damask he was thinking when he wrote: 'The rose looks fair, but fairer we it deem, For that sweet odour which doth in it live.'

COLOURWAYS FOR BOUQUET OF ROSES

PINK ROSES   Reds: A948, A941, A943, A946 (PA940, PA947, PA945, PA903)   Yellow: A843 (PA726)   Purple: A934 (PA321)

YELLOW ROSES   Yellows: A841, A996, A843 (PA715, PA762, PA726)   Reds: A622, A941, A948 (PA834, PA947, PA940)   Browns: A902, A905 (PA443, PA440)

RED ROSES   Purple: A935 (PA320)   Reds: A148, A995, A945, A943 (PA920, PA940, PA943, PA945)   Yellow: A843 (PA726)

LEAVES AND STEMS   Browns: A902, A905 (PA443, PA440)   Yellow: A475 (PA700)   Greens: A422, A402, A404, A407, A253 (PA623, PA602, PA601, PA660, PA693)

COLOURWAYS FOR SINGLE ROSE

FLOWER   Reds: A941, A708, A943, A945, A877 (PA947, PA846, PA945, PA943, PA494)   Yellows: A475, A843 (PA700, PA726)

LEAVES AND STEM   Greens: A407, A404, A402, A253 (PA660, PA601, PA602, PA693)   Browns: A905, A902 (PA440, PA443)

A CAT AND HIS CATMINT

The cat sitting here is called Fox and, like all cats, he is very important. This constant friend has prowled his way across every design I have done and slept contentedly on top of all the artwork. Muddy paws have given final touches to innumerable drawings. In the garden he watches me dig; near at hand for an occasional stroke, but never close enough to really get in the way. No needlepoint work is set up correctly until he has settled on my lap under the embroidery frame, oblivious to the dangling wool ends. In short, this grey eminence is the amber-eyed companion of my old age.

The names we give our pets often seem curious to other people. What do they tell us about ourselves or others? Would you want to meet a man who called his dog Einstein? Or a woman who called her canary Hildegarde? You might well accept an invitation to tea from an old lady who called her cat Molly, for some names are just right. For example, a hen called Flossie or Doris. Before the First World War, when farm animals were not just subsidized herds and treated as so many numbered 'food machines', farmers named their beasts with some affection. In 1908, these were some of the names given to Old Gloucester cattle: Lovely, Blossom, Beauty, Droop, Broad and Charmer. Each says something about the animal's character or what she looked like.

There is an old proverb about catmint which says, 'If you set it, the cats will eat it; if you sow it, the cats won't know it.' The cat's love for this plant, *Nepeta faassenii*, has been known since ancient times. Medieval Latin names for the plant include *herba felina*, *herba cati* and *herba cattaria*. Sometimes called catnip, it has a strong minty scent and cats like to roll in it, crushing the leaves to increase the smell, and to lie embraced by the leaves as Fox is doing in my large design. They also favour it when it is dried, hence the number of toys for cats stuffed with it.

Man has long attributed both bad and good luck to this creature. Some people think a black cat unlucky, while English sailors' wives once kept a black cat to help ensure their husbands' safe return from the sea. No doubt the connection between cats and witches grew up because the people often thought to be witches were old

The dragonfly darts over ponds, brilliant and shining in the heat of summer noon.

women living alone who frequently kept a cat for company. Some of the nicest sayings are about cats: 'When the cat's away, the mice will play'; 'A cat has nine lives'; 'A cat may look at a king'; 'The cat and the dog may kiss yet are none the better friends'; 'The cat shuts its eyes while it steals cream'. These probably tell us more about human nature than about our cats. In all folklore and old beliefs, surely none can be more in the realm of fantasy than some of the old remedies in which cats were the major ingredient. They certainly show little knowledge of a cat's behaviour and tolerance: 'To cure a stye, stroke it with the tail of a black cat'. Better still, to cure a cold, 'Stick your finger into a cat's ear for fifteen minutes'.

COLOURWAYS FOR CAT AND HIS CATMINT
CAT   Blacks: A963, A966, A998 (PA203, PA201, PA221)   White: A991B (PA260)   Red: A711 (PA914)   Yellow: A312 (PA742)
CATMINT   Purples: A603, A606 (PA313, PA310)   Greens: A354, A357 (PA602, PA600)
COLOURWAYS FOR DRAGONFLY
Red: A207 (PA871)   Purple: A884 (PA334)   Greens: A251A, A421, A524 (PA624, PA694, PA522)

LILIES WITH STRIPES

In the afternoon of the year, when old-fashioned roses have passed the full flush of their bloom, the lilies reign, standing heavily scented and solitary above most other flowers. The familiar Madonna Lily, said to have been created from milk by the Roman goddess Juno, has long been a common sight in English gardens. Shakespeare mentions it no less than twenty-eight times in his works. Besides the white lily, there are pink, mauve, orange, dark red, yellow, even a pale shade of green lily, all with a curious blend of several colours washed together around darker centres and mottled spots of colour. Lilies like to remain undisturbed, and for this reason have long been successful in the small English cottage garden, safe from strong winds, their roots tucked away among other plants in semi-shade and damp, limey soil.

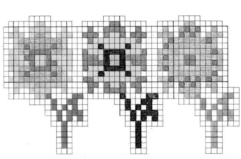

Chrysanthemum Border

The lilies in this design are *Lilium rubellum*, one of the most beautiful, and often long lasting once established. The flowers are deep pink and trumpet-shaped, and here I have emphasized the stiff posture of the lily by hot bright stripes taken from deck chairs set out in the sun.

The design may be worked as shown, or the lilies and the stripes worked as separate pieces. One lily done in the style of Victorian beadwork would be impressive. If you are over forty, get a child to thread the beading needles for you: it was once a proud custom among the best of needleworkers.

Consider the lilies of the field, how they grow; they toil not, neither do they spin: Yet I say unto you, that even Solomon in all his glory was not arrayed like one of these.

St Matthew, VI, 28

As the flower of Heaven, the lily was the symbol of purity, and so it appeared frequently throughout the centuries in samplers. In the sixteenth and seventeenth centuries, it was sometimes used as a stylized *fleur de lys* motif.

Growing throughout the northern temperate zone from China and Japan to Oregon in America, the lily is as famous in literature, art and the folklore of nations as the rose. It is the only flower mentioned by name by Jesus, although authorities do not agree that the lily was exactly the flower that was intended. Still, it has been more mentioned by poets than any other flower. Although lilies continued in popularity throughout the centuries, with the Elizabethans being especially fond of them, by the time of the Victorians, lilies had been relegated to the back row. The main reason was that there was such a stream of new and exotic flowers from abroad and such rapid cultivation of new varieties at home that people were overwhelmed with the 'new', and embroiderers did not escape this enthusiasm. With the introduction of *Lilium auratum* which was a true species from such eastern countries as Korea and Japan, the lily again became a popular garden favourite. Much of the credit for this new popularity of the lily and the development of new varieties and robust hybrids must go to the Americans. Today, there is a whole division of lilies classified as of American origin. If you would like to grow some of these but do not have space, try growing them in pots – they do well and can be brought into the house when in bloom. With their tall stems and regal look they add elegance to any room or terrace.

COLOURWAYS FOR LILIES WITH STRIPES
Reds: A752, A144, A222, A995 (PA964, PA932, PA933, PA940)   Greens: A243, A423, A357 (PA642, PA622, PA691)   Yellow: A553 (PA712)
COLOURWAYS FOR CHRYSANTHEMUM BORDER
Greens: A523, A426 (PA523, PA621)   Reds: A861, A948 (PA855, PA940)   Black: A998 (PA221)   Yellow: A551 (PA712)   Purple: A603 (PA713)

GERANIUMS

For soaps and smells, fancy beds in the garden, pots for the window-sill and old ladies' cottages, geraniums and pelargoniums are hard to beat. As if all this were not pleasing enough, geraniums are probably the easiest of all flowers to start growing – you just break off a piece and stick it in a pot of light soil. You can even start them off in a glass of water. Certainly they can get leggy and have few blooms, but with a little care they can be the flowers one sees in florists or garden centre shops – a tight mass of broad leaves and bright blooms. The ones in my design are *Geranium psilostemon*, which are a magenta-pink in colour, but there are white, pink, purple and lavender blue ones as well, and all are excellent as ground cover. Known as 'cranesbill', the common geranium can be seen growing in the wild, their saucer-shaped flowers fighting for the sun among the other wild flowers.

The small repeating background motif in the design is that embroidery favourite of a flower or leaf used without natural definition for an overall needlepoint pattern. This design, as well as a single flower or leaf from any of the patterns in the book, can be used to create large areas of needlepoint for the covering of upholstered furniture like dining chairs or armchairs. Such projects are ambitious and take a number of months, not to say years, to complete, but they do last and you are creating a heritage piece that can be passed down from generation to generation. It may last hundreds of years, given quality yarn and canvas and some discretion in use by your family.

When beginning such an important project, time is needed to plan and do the necessary preliminary work before starting the actual embroidery. You will need to make a paper pattern of the area to be covered so that you know how large the canvas is to be and the exact shape of the finished work, bearing in mind that you will need at least a two-inch margin all around for the mounting of the finished work. You should work about three extra rows of stitches on all sides as well when completing the background. These stitches will be turned under when the material is used, but they ensure that no bare canvas shows in the end product. While it is always important to try and buy sufficient background wool for a needlepoint at the time you begin it so that there is no shade variation, it is really vital to adhere to this rule when you are doing a large needlepoint which is destined for a chair or other large piece of furniture. Variations in the background of such pieces are immediately noticeable, unlike in a small cushion where shadow and shape lessen the perception of any difference.

There came a day that caught the summer
Wrung its neck
Plucked it
And ate it.

Now what shall I do with the trees?
The day said, the day said.
Strip them bare, strip them bare.
Let's see what is really there.

And what shall I do with the sun?
The day said, the day said.
Roll him away till he's cold and small.
He'll come back rested if he comes back at all.

And what shall I do with the birds?
The day said, the day said.
The birds I've frightened, let them flit,
I'll hang out pork for the brave tomtit.

And what shall I do with the seed?
The day said, the day said.
Bury it deep, see what it's worth.
See if it can stand the earth.

What shall I do with the people?
The day said, the day said.
Stuff them with apple and blackberry pie –
They'll love me then till the day they die.

There came this day and he was autumn.
His mouth was wide
And red as a sunset.
His tail was an icicle.
          'There Came a Day', Ted Hughes, 1976

COLOURWAYS FOR GERANIUMS
Reds: A862, A866, A757, A805, A946 (PA854, PA850, PA903, PA901, PA943)   Greens: A522, A426, A525 (PA524, PA621, PA522)

STRAWBERRIES

No garden would be complete without the hollyhock towering above its neighbour and giving a sense of having been planted there since time immemorial.

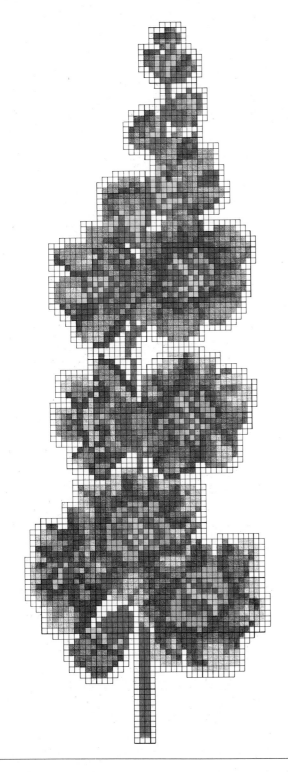

The best thing to do with strawberries is to eat them. In lieu of that, you can embroider them to enjoy for every month of the year – though as fresh strawberries are now flown around the world to your supermarket, you can probably eat them all the year as well. Why not have both needlepoint and real ones?

Curly locks, Curly locks,
  Wilt thou be mine?
Thou shalt not wash dishes
  Nor yet feed the swine.
  But sit on a cushion
  And sew a fine seam,
And feed upon strawberries,
  Sugar and cream.

Infant Institutes, 1797

The colour of the strawberry is famous, and painters and craftsmen have no monopoly, for there are strawberry roan horses, a strawberry face, referring to someone suffering from dyspepsia or high blood pressure, the strawberry pear, the bass, the cockle, the crab and the finch – to name but a few.

A strawberry may be realistically done as in a botanical study, symbolically shown for religious purposes, or embroidered as a decorative motif.

In the ancient world when the strawberry was recorded for its medicinal benefits, the leaf, fruit and roots were all shown in a highly stylized and plain manner – presumably so the reader could be easily guided to the plant in the wild. This way of showing the strawberry continued in illustrated herbals and in embroideries until well after naturalism in art became popular. It is still an attractive way to show this favourite fruit.

COLOURWAYS FOR STRAWBERRY REPEAT
STRAWBERRIES   Reds: A995, A944, A941 (PA840, PA944, PA947)
LEAVES AND STEMS   Green: A429 (PA620)   Black: A993 (PA220)
COLOURWAYS FOR HOLLYHOCK
Purples: A106, A606, A604, A601 (PA310, PA312, PA313, PA314)   Reds: A622, A995, A148 (PA834, PA840, PA920)   Yellow: A844 (PA702)   Greens: A253, A358 (PA693, PA610)

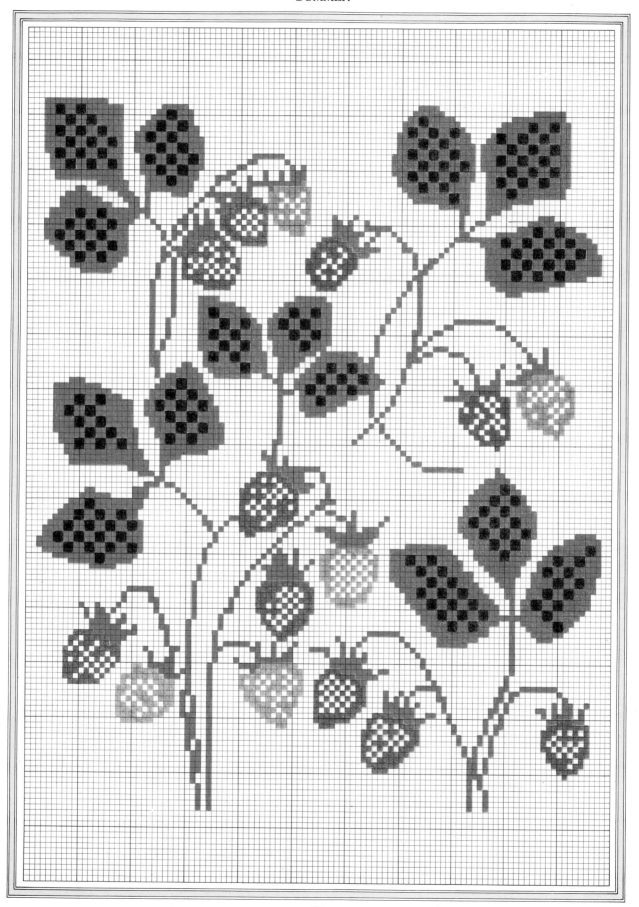

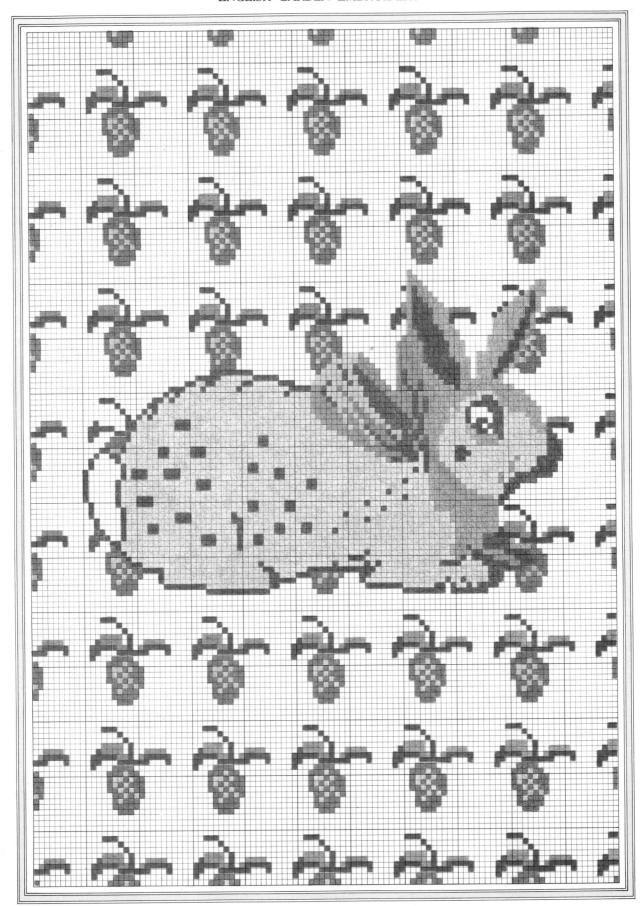

RABBIT IN A BERRY PATCH

In a suburban town garden, you would be surprised to find a rabbit in your cabbage patch, let alone among your strawberries. In a country garden it is a different matter, and these cute little creatures can do a lot of damage. Looking down into the far part of my garden beyond where I have fenced it, I can see rabbits nibbling about in the early evening. There are never very many and they do little harm it seems to me, for the fields around the place give them more than ample herbage. Once in a while, if everything is very quiet, a hare will appear – large, powerful, and increasingly rare. The rabbits, unlike the hare, always look domesticated; I suppose this is because we keep them as pets and every child is raised on the stories of that most famous rabbit, Peter.

By 1925 there were 1,362 cultivated varieties of strawberries available in the United States. Today that list has grown on both sides of the Atlantic with many of the old varieties being dropped and better new ones added every year. Since Victorian days, the main aim of strawberry breeders has been to obtain fruit of uniform size and simultaneously ready to harvest. In his book *Plants and Plant Life* (1954), Edgar Anderson had no hesitation in declaring that the new strains of strawberry are 'the one crop of world importance to have originated in modern times'. Varieties suitable for growing in Britain are not usually right for America, though those from America's eastern seaboard may do well in Britain and vice versa. Some new American varieties like Totem and Shasta have done remarkably well in Britain.

Vegetables and fruits can be as decorative in the garden as flowers. A strawberry barrel can be sited on a patio or terrace, as the centrepiece in a small town garden, or just outside the kitchen door. Its continuous flowers

and berries will be as bright as a small bed of summer flowers – and give you pounds of delicious fruit into the bargain. The berries will remain clean and dry and beyond the reach of slugs.

You can use summer-fruiting strawberries or perpetuals – Gento is a good choice. You can, of course, mix varieties to give a long harvest and display season.

The only work after planting is to pinch out runners and weed the top. Remember that your summer slogan must be 'Constant watering'.

Besides the strawberry barrel, other good containers include vertical-display 'towerpots', which hold up to twelve plants, are easily watered and make a pretty show. Ordinary earthenware and plastic pots will do the job too – in fact, any container works so long as it is kept well watered.

In the first place the strawberry's chief need is a great deal of water. In the second place, it needs more water. In the third place, I think I would give it a great deal more water.
Laxton Brothers' *Strawberry Manual*,
Marshall Wilder, 1899

COLOURWAYS FOR RABBIT IN A BERRY PATCH
RABBIT   Browns: A301, A303, A305 (PA411, PA483, PA404)   White: A991 (PA261)
RIBBON   Reds: A866, A623, A621 (PA854, PA852, PA850)
STRAWBERRIES   Reds: A504, A754 (PA950, PA905)
LEAVES   Greens: A424, A429 (PA662, PA620)

COLOURWAYS FOR STRAWBERRY BORDER
Reds: A504, A754 (PA950, PA905)   Greens: A424, A429 (PA662, PA620)

SUMMER TIME

'Summertime – and the living is easy' goes the song. In the garden, given a decent English summer, it can be true, with every nook and cranny in bloom and leaf. The bounty is so great that a regular supply of bouquets for the house is in order. This large design of just such a bouquet has as many flowers as I could squeeze onto the page. There are morning glories, zinnias, rosebuds, poppies, day-lilies, pinks, cosmos, a passion flower, tobacco plant flowers, a twig of hypericum, blue flax, lilies in a wishful blue, and a thistle which should not have been in the garden at all.

Butterflies do come into the house and may stop off at your drive-in restaurant bouquet until they find an open window and go back to the garden. The little butterfly in the large design can be used on other needlepoint pieces, her colours changed as you wish.

COLOURWAYS FOR SUMMER TIME
BOUQUET AND BUTTERFLY   Reds: A752, A622, A148, A714, A441, A626, A995, A502, A442 (PA934, PA834, PA920, PA912, PA823, PA830, PA840, PA971, PA822)   Browns: A913, A902, A696, A905 (PA712, PA443, PA752, PA440)   Yellows: A843, A553 (PA726, PA712)   Purples: A884, A103, A935 (PA313, PA311, PA320)   Blues: A461, A464, A326, A322 (PA546, PA542, PA511, PA514)   Black: A998 (PA221)   Greens: A253, A435, A431, A423, A427, A407, A404 (PA693, PA683, PA687, PA622, PA696, PA660, PA601)
COLOURWAYS FOR GARDEN URN
Browns: A204, A724, A725 (PA860, PA862, PA405)

Large urns such as this one can be seen in many of the large formal gardens of English stately homes. Such a design framed by a simple border could be used as the pattern for needlepoint chair covers.

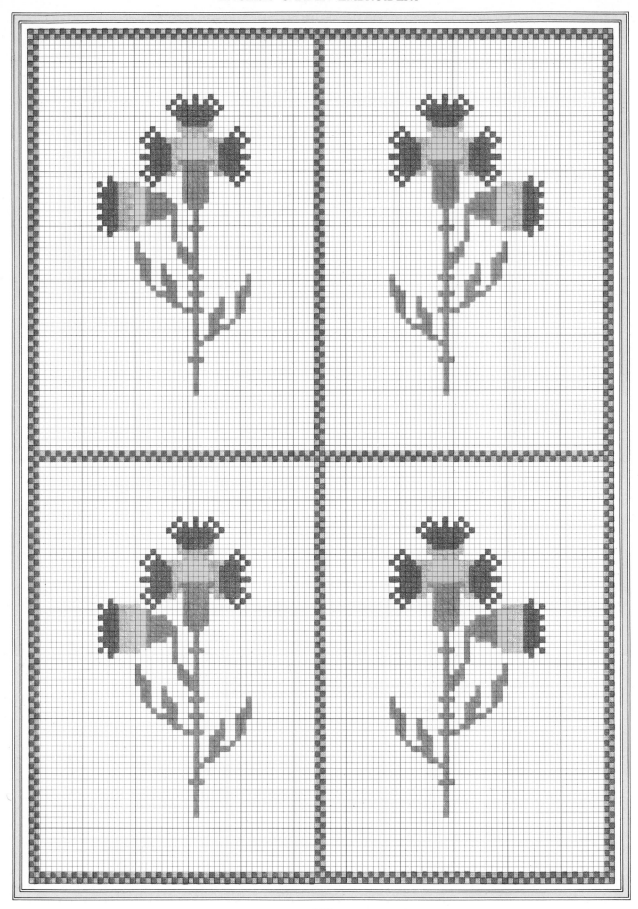

CARNATIONS

In the seventeenth century poets and writers were very aware of embroideries, and John Milton's observations in 1637 on the motifs in a needlepoint sum up the many flowers that were familiar and beloved by embroiderers of his time. High among these were the carnation and pink.

Bring the rathe primrose that forsaken dies,
The tufted crow-toe, the pale jessamine,
The white pink, the pansy freakt with jet,
The glowing violet,
The musk-rose, and the well attir'd woodbine,
With cowslips wan that hang the pensive head,
And every flower that sad embroidery wears.

The carnations in my large design are based on the kind likely to have been found in samplers of the eighteenth century. The repeating band of carnations in the small design is based on seventeenth-century ones. There is much to commend the earlier embroidery practice of doing stylized flowers such as these carnations.

The carnation was the most esteemed of Rome's flowers, being named 'Flower of Jupiter'. It was used for garlands and coronets and its name meant coronation and, hence, carnation, in early English. When the English, before the nineteenth century, referred to a gillyflower, they probably meant in most instances the carnation and pink. These flowers have the scent of cloves and as the summer air becomes hot so this perfume drifts up from the pathways along my garden where they are planted. Carnations are divided into three divisions which are fancifully named: the *Flakes*, which have stripes going through the petals; the *Bizarres*, which are of two colours;

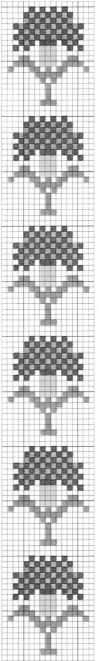

and, finally, my favourite one, the *Picotees*, which have a white ground edged with red, rose or purple. Just two carnations or a small handful of their diminutive relation, the pink, in a vase will give a notable perfume to a room.

He who bathes in May, will soon be laid in clay; he who bathes in June, will sing a merry tune.

Old Saying

English gardeners had the pleasure of receiving many new varieties of flowers and plants from the New World, especially America. One of the most famous early Americans whose interest in gardening helped to create a steady exchange of flowers and food plants was Thomas Jefferson (1743-1826), third president of the United States and chief author of that country's Declaration of Independence. He was not only an outstanding patriot in the cause of freedom but a plantsman of note. His *Garden Notebooks* which he kept over the years to record his observations, his harvests and his plantings, show how well he tried to cater for others with gifts of new seed, special requests for this or that medicinal plant, and new botanical information and plants. He wrote of himself:

I have often thought that if heaven had given me choice of my position and calling, it should have been on a rich spot of earth, well watered, and near a good market for the production of the garden. No occupation is so delightful to me as the culture of the soil.

COLOURWAYS FOR CARNATIONS
Reds: A502, A752 (PA971, PA964) Green: A425 (PA698) Yellow: A552 (PA773)
COLOURWAYS FOR CARNATION
BORDER   As above

ROSE GEOMETRIC

European art abounds with human figures, landscapes and objects of everyday living, but from the Islamic countries comes the most elaborate of geometric art – the abstraction of lines into complex and beautiful patterns. The English garden also contains such geometric designs: brick paths, mazes, edgings for borders, trellis, fencing of every sort, and even the shapes of trees, shrubs and other plants. The roundness of stems and trunks translates into circles, and the patterns on leaves and the surface of petals provide more designs. If you begin by drawing a few lines over each other or overlapping two circles, you can repeat such motifs endlessly, giving rise to hundreds of different patterns. Merely altering a curve or an angle of a line immediately creates a new pattern. Try drawing four lines down and across, putting a square in each box, and you have created a geometric design.

In this design, Rose Geometric, the natural rose is combined with an abstract block pattern. It is based on an old piece of fabric in the collection of Stanley Duller of Moreton-in-Marsh, who is a professional embroiderer.

The combination of a familiar object such as a rose with a geometric repeat is almost always pleasing, for the flower softens the harder lines of the geometric.

It is important to keep strict count of stitches in doing this kind of pattern.

Out through the fields and the woods
And over the walls I have wended;
I have climbed the hills of view
And looked at the world, and descended;
I have come by the highway home,
And lo, it is ended.

The leaves are all dead on the ground,
Save those that the oak is keeping
To ravel them one by one
And let them go scraping and creeping
Out over the crusted snow,
When others are sleeping.

And the dead leaves lie huddled and still,
No longer blown hither and thither;
The last lone aster is gone;
The flowers of the witch hazel wither;
The heart is still aching to seek,
But the feet question 'Whither?'

Ah, when to the heart of man
Was it ever less than a treason
To go with the drift of things,
To yield with a grace to reason
And bow and accept the end
Of a love or a season?
'Reluctance', Robert Frost, 1875-1963

The morning glory, blue convolvulus, closes its flowers at about 4 o'clock to tell you it is time for tea.

COLOURWAYS FOR ROSE GEOMETRIC
Reds: A864, A759, A943, A946, A948 (PA853, PA900, PA945, PA903, PA940)   Blues: A748, A565, A741, A745 (PA501, PA583, PA505, PA503)   Purples: A603, A607 (PA313, PA310)   Browns: A315, A313, A334 (PA471, PA741, PA730)   Greens: A421, A423, A426, A253, A255, A358 (PA624, PA622, PA621, PA693, PA691, PA610)   White: A992 (PA262)
COLOURWAYS FOR MORNING GLORY
FLOWERS   Blues: A464, A465, A462 (PA543, PA545, PA540)   Reds: A502, A623, A752 (PA971, PA834, PA964)
LEAVES   Greens: A545, A543, A548 (PA661, PA611, PA610)

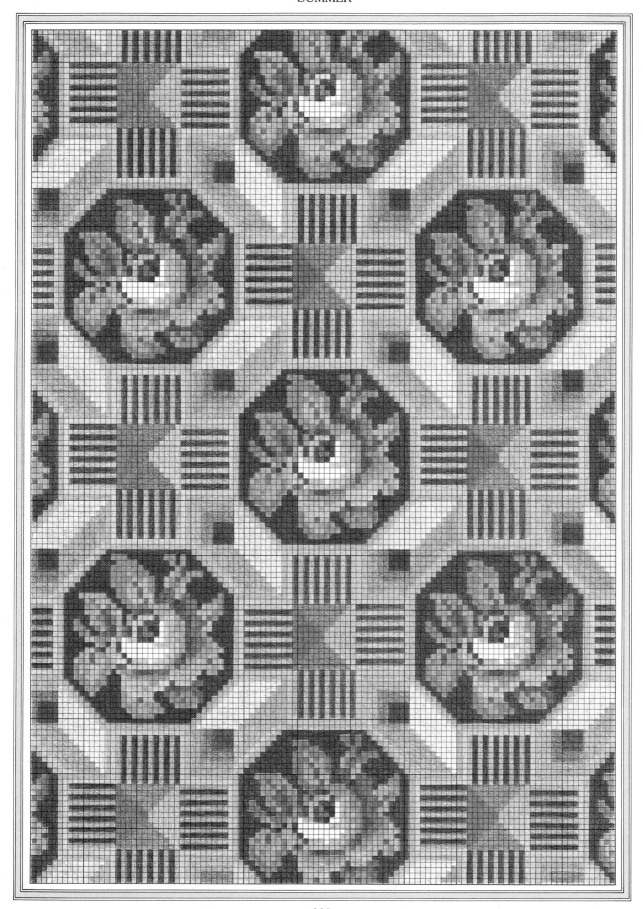

BUTTERFLIES

In England the most spectacular butterflies appear during July and August, and red admirals, commas, whites, peacocks, and tortoiseshells mean the garden has become a huge feeding ground, especially if it has red valerian, buddleia, sedum, daisies, honeysuckle and lavender, all high on the preferred menus of the butterfly. It is now that the intimate community of insects and plants are engaged in their intricate relationship of mutual benefit and mutual exploitation.

With the proliferation of weed killers and other chemical sprays, butterflies like other insects have suffered. Happily, many gardeners now make a conscious effort to promote butterflies in their gardens – not just for their beauty but to help foster the survival of this most charming of garden visitors. The standard food which we can easily provide them is *Buddleia davidii*, the butterfly plant, with its long graceful cascades of flowers. It dies back in a hard winter, but given just a little protection such as being near a wall, it will thrive. This tall flowering plant can be matched in fragrance for our pleasure and in food for the butterflies by heliotrope, or what the English call 'cherry pie'. This flower smells of vanilla, and it is this evocative scent that butterflies and humans seem to love. Butterflies enjoy a wide choice in their flower preferences, so even if you do not consider them when you are planning your garden, they are apt to arrive. As to colour of flower, some butterflies may like yellow-blue at the beginning of their life cycle and change to red-blue as they mature. Surviving is a hallmark of the insect world and butterflies are no exception in spite of their beauty, so in addition to flowers, they will feed on fallen fermenting fruit, honeydew, bird droppings and dung.

One of the world's most interesting naturalists is Miriam Rothschild. Her experiments in cultivating crops of wild flowers and introducing them back into appropriate existing grasslands have resulted in an entirely new venture for farmers in England. She has contributed much to today's trend to conserve native flora and fauna. When she writes of her own sentiments about butterflies in her book *The Butterfly Gardener*, she sums up the feelings most of us have about these pretty 'floating flowers':
'I garden purely for pleasure. I love plants and flowers and green leaves and I am incurably romantic – hankering after small stars spangling the grass. Butterflies add another dimension to the garden for they are like dream flowers – childhood dreams – which have broken loose from their stalks and escaped into the sunshine. Air and angels. This is the way I look upon their presence.'

In the large design, I have shown a number of butterflies, mostly coloured from imagination, against green leaves. The darker the leaves, the more these butterflies will appear as little jewels on your embroidery. You can place a butterfly in almost any needlepoint of flowers. I do them in embroidery silk over the top of the wool needlepoint.

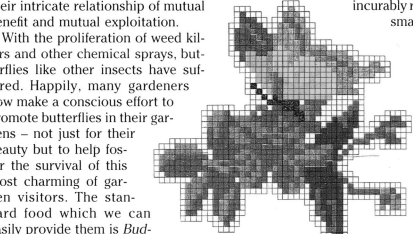

A Butterfly on a Flower.

COLOURWAYS FOR BUTTERFLIES
BUTTERFLIES   Yellows: A695, A551 (PA751, PA773)   Green: A334 (PA742)   Brown: A313 (PA730)   Blacks: A963, A966, A998 (PA203, PA201, PA221)   Reds: A759, A946, A864, A861 (PA900, PA903, PA853, PA855)   Blues: A712, A745, A741, A748 (PA553, PA503, PA505, PA501)
LEAVES   Greens: A338, A407, A354, A356 (PA450, PA660, PA610, PA602)
BORDER   A861, A864 (PA855, PA853)
COLOURWAYS FOR BUTTERFLY ON A FLOWER
BUTTERFLY   Brown: A304 (PA411)   Blues: A741, A745 (PA505, PA503)   Yellows: A843, A311 (PA734, PA726)
FLOWER   Reds: A943, A948, A864 (PA945, PA940, PA853)   Greens: A426, A421 (PA621, PA622)

SUNFLOWERS

The common sunflower, native to Mexico and Peru and a familiar sight in many gardens, was once called Marigold of Peru in England. A traditional cottage and urban garden flower, children find it easy and fun to grow. The important thing for them is seeing how tall their sunflower can grow – the record is 23½ feet. Some communities today run a special 'Tallest Sunflower Competition' each summer to raise money for charity.

Ah, Sun-flower! weary of time,
Who countest the steps of the sun,
Seeking after that sweet golden clime
Where the traveller's journey is done:

Where the youth pined away with desire,
And the pale virgin shrouded in snow
Arise from their graves, and aspire
Where my Sun-flower wishes to go.
              'The Sun-Flower', William Blake, 1757-1827

This handsome and vigorous plant with its broad leaves and sunny face bursting with seeds is a good friend to mankind. Every part of the plant can be utilized for some purpose: the leaves are good for cattle fodder; the stems are useful in the process of making paper; the seed is rich in oil; and the flowers and petals contain a yellow dye. Sunflower oil is now widely used, especially by those trying to reduce their intake of oils and foods high in polysaturated fats. The oil has a slightly sweet taste and can be used as an adequate substitute for olive and almond oils. I say 'adequate', because every oil *is* different from another.

The cake left from pressing the seeds for oil yields a less valuable non-cooking oil which is then used as a lubricant. Even the residue after all the oil is finally pressed out is useful, for it is formed into cakes and fed to cattle, sheep, pigs, pigeons, rabbits and poultry. Chickens devour sunflower seeds with the greatest greed and just three or four plants in the garden will bring you a harvest to last your chickens through the winter.

We can eat the seeds, of course, along with the chickens. The people of Russia and India are especially fond of roasted sunflower seeds in their cooking, and most modern organic and natural foods and vegetarian cook books con-

tain recipes for using the seeds either raw or roasted. Such recipes range from sunflower butter, which is rather like peanut butter, to seed biscuits, carrots with sunflower seeds, Waldorf salad dressing and vegetable crumble.

Had I the heavens' embroider'd cloths,
Enwrought with golden and silver light,
The blue and the dim and the dark cloths
Of night and light and the half light,
I would spread the cloths under your feet:
But I, being poor, have only my dreams;
I have spread my dreams under your feet;
Tread softly because you tread on my dreams.
              'He Wishes for the Cloths of Heaven',
                      William Butler Yeats, 1865-1939

Sunflower seeds are one of the most nourishing foods readily available to us, growing just outside our kitchen door. They are an outstanding source of essential fatty acids and protein, containing vital nutrients, most of the vitamins B, vitamin E, and pound for pound twice as much iron and twenty-five times as much thiamin as a steak. Research has shown that chewing the seeds will lessen the desire to smoke and, thus, can help you reduce or give up cigarettes if you are addicted to them. Apparently the seeds contain ingredients which mimic some of the effects of nicotine itself.

As if this were not enough, the handsome sunflower holding its head up in the sky toward the summer sun supplies linoleic acid, which has been used in the treatment of multiple sclerosis.

It seems fitting to close the summer season of embroidery design on this most valuable of garden flowers and one which more than any other proclaims to gardener and artist alike that summer is a time of rejoicing in the beauty and bounty of nature.

COLOURWAYS FOR SUNFLOWERS
FLOWERS   Yellows: A551, A553, A844 (PA773, PA712, PA702)   Brown: A187 (PA451)   Purple: A601 (PA474)   White: A992 (PA262)
LEAVES AND STEMS   Greens: A358, A427, A544, A422 (PA610, PA696, PA612, PA623)   Black: A998 (PA221)

Welcome to you, rich Autumn days,
    Ere comes the cold, leaf-picking wind;
When golden stocks are seen in fields,
    All standing arm-in-arm entwined;
And gallons of sweet cider seen
On trees in apples red and green.

With mellow pears that cheat our teeth,
    Which melt that tongues may suck them in;
With blue-black damsons, yellow plums,
    Now sweet and soft from stone to skin;
And woodnuts rich, to make us go
Into the loneliest lanes we know.
                'Rich Days', W. H. Davies, 1871-1940

AUTUMN

How quietly and unobserved late summer slips into autumn. September arrives with its abundance of blooms and the promise of asters, Michaelmas daisies, pretty-leaved hostas, golden rod – the last of the bright yellows of the year in my garden – and the early chrysanthemums. Before we know it, fruits that often ripen late are asking to be eaten – apricots, if you have a warm south wall, and peaches too. Grapes hang in clusters telling us that summer has been hot or too cool. For those who have eaten their fill of figs in the Mediterranean, the idea that we can pick some now from our own English gardens seems like wishful thinking.

Yet figs are an old-time fruit in England and, from summer to summer, we do have enough hot days to ripen the varieties that can do well in our climate. It is necessary to restrict the roots if you want any fruit and, in Britain, figs don't usually ripen north of the Trent River. 'White Marseilles' and 'Brown Turkey' are highly recommended varieties to plant. The former has almost white fruit when ripe and the latter, figs that are green-brown and don't at all resemble their blue-black sisters of the southern countries. Whether they ripen their fruit or not, their display of broad dense leaves is handsome in a garden.

A few years ago I embroidered a cushion as a gift which had only red fruit motifs – apples, cherries, strawberries, redcurrants and raspberries. You don't have to be very skilled to make each of these look like it should. The shapes are there in nature and are very different from each other. Try drawing the outline of an apple, a pear, some blackberries, or other fruits from the autumn garden; then interpret these shapes in wool.

There are blackberries and many other fruits to be gathered during autumn, some from the garden, some from the orchard, some in the hedgerows. But we are not the only busy ones in this annual harvest. The mice are there and many insects, including wasps – landing, rising, angry with temptations and immediately possessive of everything honeyed, rich and desirable on our harvest table. And it is to the table the wasp *will* come, uninvited and rude, settling on the rim of a jar, plugging itself into ripe fruit, stalking the edge of a plate smeared with new jam.

In the English garden we have digger wasps and true wasps. The true wasps are of two kinds, solitary and social. Aptly named, it is the social ones that come to tea-tables and picnics. We panic when they appear but, in truth, they are not very aggressive and will not sting unless provoked. I am never certain what is meant by 'provocative action' in the insect world, but I suppose waving your arms about is a bad idea. Don't kill wasps, for they serve us well by destroying a variety of garden insect pests.

Many flower arrangers seem to be inspired by what is available to them in the autumn. Perhaps nature is more in command of the colour in summer, for it seems no matter what mixture of flowers you gather the final result is either bright or ends in a single colour theme. Autumn is another story, for the colours soften now, the choice of flowers forces greater discernment

Ehret's *Jargonelle Pear*.

and the changing colours of leaves begins to inspire more novel arrangements. The bright pink of nerines, rosy sedums and the varigated hosta leaves make a fine selection not only to arrange but to embroider.

With the upright chrysanthemums, rigid sedums, straight golden rod, and the branches and twigs of bushes and small trees, structure and form is more definitive. All the flopping roses are gone, although there will be a last-minute fling of blooms. I call it 'a last goodbye to summer' and take in the garden furniture.

With the low pink and rust-coloured sedum, and the waving wands of white, purple, orange-eyed blues or mauve flowers of the buddleia, the butterflies shower themselves over my garden. During the summer, there have been many among the flowers and vegetables. Now they drink as at a banquet, recovering on warm walls and bricks and then dancing up again in crazy patterns.

As aromatic plants bestow
No spicy fragrance while they grow,
But crush'd or trodden to the ground,
Diffuse their balmy sweets around.
             Oliver Goldsmith, ?1730-1774

There are always a few last bouquets in an autumn garden. I have included two of my old-fashioned, Victorian-type designs which can be as bright or as sombre as the wool colours in which you may choose to do them. A bouquet in the garden at this time of the year may be odd little late-summer flowers, a nice rose, the smallest ends of buddleia, some asters and blue stars of borage.

An older kind of bouquet can be gathered in the garden now as well as during late summer, one that lasts long and arouses memories of wood smoke and the fragrant winter food to come. This bouquet is a tussie-mussie, a gathering of tiny twigs of thyme and rosemary, leaves of lemon balm and scented geranium with a rose bud at the centre of the arrangement.

Tussie-mussies were originally carried by ladies to help protect them against diseases, and were normally made of sweet-smelling herbs. The name is an old one, going back as far as 1440, and in Victorian times they were sent, with flower bouquets and nosegays, to someone you loved, each flower or herb standing for a word, emotion or letter of the alphabet to spell out a message. The tussie-mussie has come back into favour with the renewed popularity of herbs in the garden. It is a thoughtful gift to bring an elderly or ill friend who may not want the overwhelming smell of florists' flowers in a small room.

It is easy to make a tussie-mussie. First take a rosebud and arrange around it some frilly foliage like silver artemesia. Tie this up with some light thread and leave a long end of the thread hanging down to be used as you gather in more items to the bouquet. Surround the rosebud centre piece with circle after circle of herbs – rosemary, marjoram, thyme, lavender and mint. (I find borage unsuitable for tussie-mussies as it is sticky.)

As you add each herb, bind it in with the thread so that you create a nosegay. To finish your tussie-mussie, surround it with a final circle of scented geranium leaves or variegated sage. Tie it up with the remaining thread so that it all stays together. The charm of tussie-mussies lie in the fact that no two ever look alike. This sweet-smelling nosegay is, of course, perfectly edible. Having enjoyed one for a week in the sitting-room, I have snipped the wet bottoms off and given it burial as flavouring for a stew.

Onions, garlic, cloves, walnuts, grapes, apples, parsley, chives, thyme, juniper berries and chestnuts are just some of the harvest to put with the new food of autumn. You may be lucky and be able to gather many of these ingredients from your own garden. If you live, as I do, in a very rural area endowed with much game, then the game can be got too – hare, partridge, wild duck, quail, pheasant and pigeon. For myself, I like watching most of these creatures too much to eat them. I allow one tough old pheasant to pick his way daily back and forth across pastures and garden to arrive in his red mask and long coat tail at my barn door to seek fallen grain. 'Best in the oven', French friends would cry! When the garlic is hanging up in the kitchen, the onions and herbs all in from the garden, the taste for that old bird is hard to resist.

Let onion atoms lurk within the bowl
And, half suspected, animate the whole.
                          Sydney Smith, 1771-1845

Smell, above all other senses, remains for me the outstanding feature of autumn, as my garden begins her journey into rest and renewal. But before all this happens, there are lots of other things to harvest – the orange and green Chinese lanterns, for example, perfectly shaped with their small bell fruit inside. Strip off the leaves and hang the stems to dry beside long stiff lengths of *Achillea* 'Gold Plate' and branches of thin shining discs of 'silver dollars'. You have the makings here of a colourful display for the house that will last out the winter.

October begins the real season of leaves which lasts until the end of November, the close of the three autumnal months. There are nuts to gather before the grey squirrels get going. Even a modest cottage usually has at least a filbert in its garden. Grander places and old rectories may boast of a walnut tree.

It would be impossible to list all the colours of autumn leaves, for they may be as red as blood, or orange, copper, pink, all shades of green, gold and yellow, purple and blue. The shapes of the leaves alter as they come to earth: folded, flat, frayed, lace-edged from the wind, curled up, sometimes with an insect already asleep inside. We may rejoice in spring and delight in summer but in autumn, nature shows us decay and change and ending. Then, mindful of the ages of man, we may grow sad and need to remember that 'life and death are two locked caskets each of which contains the key to the other'.

Margaret, are you grieving
Over Goldengrove unleaving?
Leaves like the things of man, you
With your fresh thoughts care for, can you?
Ah! as the heart grows older
It will come to such sights colder
By and by, nor spare a sigh
Though worlds of wanwood leafmeal lie;
And yet you will weep and know why.
Now no matter, child, the name:
Sorrow's springs are the same.
Nor mouth had, no nor mind, expressed
What heart heard of, ghost guessed:
It is the blight man was born for,
It is Margaret you mourn for.
                'Spring and Fall – to a young child',
                Gerard Manley Hopkins, 1844-1889

PEARS

Could the pear in its autumn gold be the famous 'apple' Paris awarded to Aphrodite? Surely this lush reward at the end of summer is meant to bring nothing but pleasure. While apples are an evergreen motif in decorative art I couldn't resist taking pears as a large design for needlepoint.

Although pears do not appear to have had any particular symbolic importance in former times, since they do not have a biblical role, they are found in much art. In medieval times the pear was the most popular fruit after the apple and the two fruits have always gone together, harvested as they were at the same time. Both were eaten in the same way – tarts and pies, baked or stewed. Pears were used more often in cooking than apples. Old varieties of pears were hard to eat raw but perfect if cooked.

Pears poached in wine is one of my favourite desserts. You can do them in either red or white wine. Use some lemon peel with white wine and put in a tablespoon of honey.

'An apple pie without some cheese is like a kiss without a squeeze.'

PEARS BAKED IN RED WINE
Those with solid-fuel stoves are lucky for this dish needs a very slow oven.

Peel the pears but leave on the stalks. Put in a heavy pot. Add 3 oz (75 g) vanilla sugar per pound of pears. Half-fill with red wine and top up with enough water to cover the pears. Bake in a slow oven for between six and seven hours. The pears will be juicy and there should be little liquid left. To keep the pears from going too dark and dry on the sides exposed to air as the wine reduces, turn them over in the liquid from time to time as they cook. To serve, pile the pears on a dish and bring to the table when cold accompanied by a side dish of thick cream.

The pear is found in early embroidery and in many samplers but usually as a single-motif item and not in the more stylized repeating patterns of embroidered bands. In Victorian times, all the fruits became embroidery objects but were often put together in great baskets, or in rather stilted still-life scenes, imitative of paintings. There are still many examples around of fruit embroidered in wool, silk or in beads, and any number of those done in raised work, padded out with extraordinary skill and made as life-like as possible.

Whether or not an apple a day keeps anything away is doubtful, but the folklore is so much more comforting than most of the reports from the world of modern medicine that I think we should count apples and any other unsprayed raw food as good fortune. I have provided only one design of an apple – round, pink, red and green, with two leaves and a bit of twig at the top. It is a plain honest chap.

COLOURWAYS FOR PEARS
PEARS Yellows: A552, A695 (PA727, PA704) Reds: A626, A844, A862 (PA752, PA834, PA851) Green: A311 (PA726)
LEAVES Greens: A241, A243, A311 (PA691, PA693, PA726)
STEMS Green: A256 (PA660)
COLOURWAYS FOR APPLE
APPLE Reds: A864, A946, A948 (PA864, PA951, PA840) Greens: A253, A254 (PA670, PA692)
LEAVES AND STEM Greens: A543, A546 (PA653, PA690) Browns: A764, A766 (PA401, PA722)

LAST BOUQUETS

There are always a few last bouquets to be gathered in the autumn garden. In fact, I find I can put together a few flowers, buds, berries, leaves and small branches at any time of the year. Until the snow really blankets everything, there are few excuses for not having a bouquet or arrangement in the house.

This design for two little bouquets is highly stylized. The larger one may strike you as bud- or tulip-shaped, but it is simply a flower shape. The leaves are formal. Both motifs could be used separately in another design or the larger one might be placed in the centre with the small motif repeated around it. The medallion framing each motif in my design can also be used separately. Whether they frame anything or not is up to you. You could put different colours in each medallion, or embroider the initials of a loved one in the central medallion. As to the style of lettering for the initials, I should look about for an older, Victorian script. The Victorians were much given to monogramming everything from slippers and dressing-gowns to handkerchiefs and gloves. They produced some fancy scrolled alphabet letters and you can find a number of modern publications, mostly American, that have reproduced these.

My mother bids me bind my hair
With bands of rosy hue,
Tie up my sleeves with ribbons rare,
And lace my bodice blue.
'My Mother Bids Me Bind My Hair',
Anne Hunter, 1742-1821

Ribbons are among the most delightful things to see in needlepoint, but they can be an aggravation to work because of the seemingly endless changes of wool colours. If you work ahead in one colour, the pattern count always goes awry, and the result is much pulling out of wool since you can't cheat it – a ribbon being exact in its curls and turns, and dark and light shades. This design is shown as a group of ribbons hanging down the page. In reality, you would most likely use one continuously down the canvas.

A ribbon design makes an excellent cover for a Victorian nursing chair, where you need only cover the back and the seat. This lends itself to the vertical or horizontal lines of ribbons.

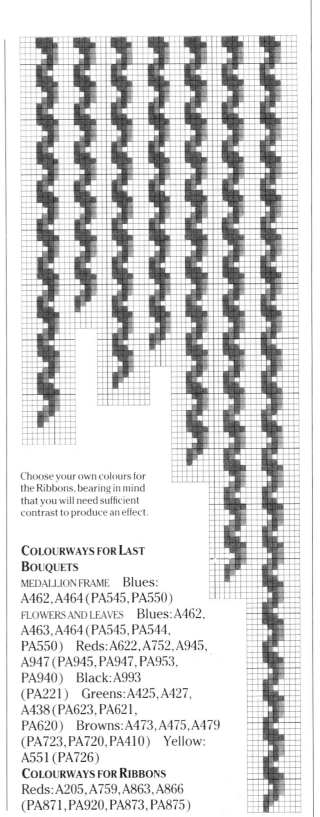

Choose your own colours for the Ribbons, bearing in mind that you will need sufficient contrast to produce an effect.

COLOURWAYS FOR LAST BOUQUETS

MEDALLION FRAME Blues: A462, A464 (PA545, PA550)
FLOWERS AND LEAVES Blues: A462, A463, A464 (PA545, PA544, PA550)   Reds: A622, A752, A945, A947 (PA945, PA947, PA953, PA940)   Black: A993 (PA221)   Greens: A425, A427, A438 (PA623, PA621, PA620)   Browns: A473, A475, A479 (PA723, PA720, PA410)   Yellow: A551 (PA726)

COLOURWAYS FOR RIBBONS
Reds: A205, A759, A863, A866 (PA871, PA920, PA873, PA875)

BLACKBERRIES AND THISTLE

In early September, the giggling you hear behind a hedgerow is more likely to be children gathering blackberries than secret lovers. When I lived in Oxfordshire I often watched a neighbour's three sons gather berries in plastic buckets. Much yelling was followed by long minutes of concentration as each tried to find the biggest or what he thought was a prize berry. Size definitely counts when you are ten years old. Later, they would stand at the lane corner with a sign saying 'Farm Fresh Berries', the berries slowly turning into juice at the bottom of their pails as the afternoon wore on.

The unusual feature of the blackberry is that it has blossoms and fruit at various stages of ripening all at the same time, unlike almost all other plants. As soon as a blossom is out, it seems to hurry to turn it into fruit. In the design

for blackberries I have shown them massed over the whole pattern and in stylized form, again using the black stitches to reinforce the folk-art quality as I have done in the designs for strawberries and for grapes.

The colours of blackberries vary from the rich purple-black of the very ripe ones to pale reds and greens of those still ripening. The white and pink blooms are scattered here and there as shoots entwine themselves through the hedgerows.

The blackberry is a graceful plant and useful to man and beast – its leaves are a stimulating tonic for farmyard stock. When I watch animals grazing on uncultivated land and along the hedgerows, I wonder how it is that Western man has lost his ability to pick and choose plants, herbs and leaves from nature's own store of such things. Is it that we no longer listen to our own bodies or is there yet another sense, perhaps the sixth one, which creatures retain and we have lost?

There are cotton thistles, holy thistles, woolly-headed thistles, melancholy thistles, dwarf ones, and musk, spear, plume and star thistles.

The deserted moor where I live is full of several of these varieties and yet I planted some special plants in my garden, *Cirsium rivulare atropurpureum*, which look exactly like thistles too. These are tall with red flowers and are very much the aristocrat at the back of a border.

The small design shown here is for the common thistle we all recognize – violet-, lavender- and mauve-coloured with touches of red, and the familiar spiky, jagged leaves.

COLOURWAYS FOR BLACKBERRIES
BLOSSOMS   Red: A942 (PA955)
BERRIES   Purples: A603, A712, A716 (PA313, PA322, PA900)
LEAVES   Green: A402 (PA612)   Black: A993 (PA220)
BORDER   Purples: A712, A716 (PA322, PA900)
COLOURWAYS FOR THISTLE
FLOWERS   Purples: A101, A103 (PA313, PA310)   Reds: A503, A505 (PA841, PA940)
LEAVES AND STEM   Greens: A831, A833, A835 (PA665, PA663, PA661)

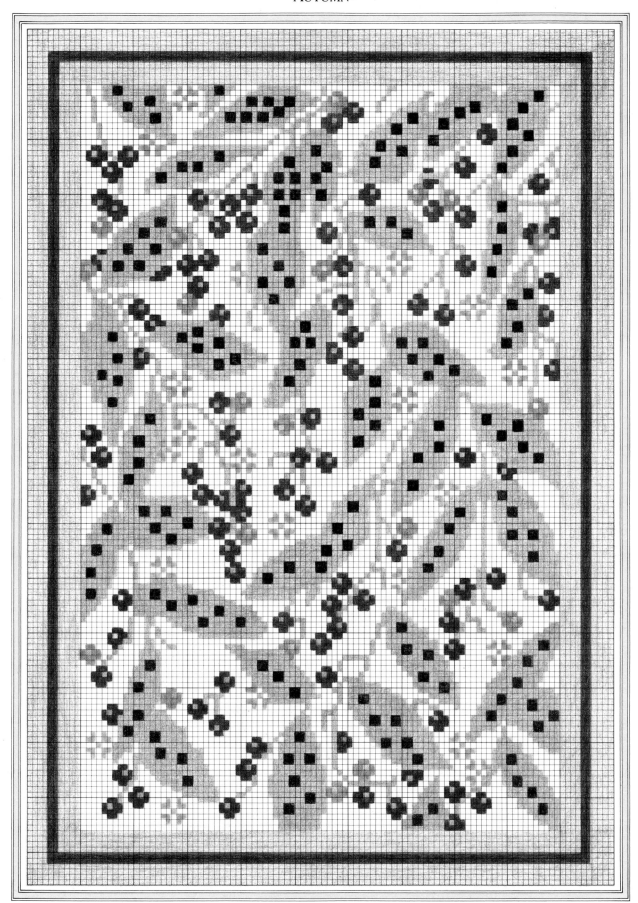

LITTLE OWL

When night comes there are many visitors to the garden and none more distinguished than the owl. There is an old German saying that 'the world likes to have night-owls, that it may have matter for wonder'. His cries are so similar to the human voice that we have long considered the owl to be something very special and a symbol of great wisdom.

The idea that, after death, the soul leaves the body in the form of a bird occurs in many different cultures over thousands of years. This belief, coupled with the owl's human-like appearance, due to his flat face with its binocular vision, probably accounts for man's long-held suspicion that this bird is a supernatural being and the embodiment of a god.

We may think such old beliefs foolish, but they persist in our culture and, therefore, in our lives. The ancient Greeks believed the owl belonged to Athene, goddess of wisdom. The Romans borrowed this tradition and gave the owl to their goddess of wisdom, Minerva, who, they thought, turned into an owl when she travelled.

A wise old owl sat in an oak;
The more he saw, the less he spoke;
The less he spoke, the more he heard.
Why aren't we like that wise old bird?

Old Proverb

The owl has been present in all European cultures thereafter, whether as witch's companion or as prophet of the weather. If it is bad weather when the owl hoots, it means the weather will improve. In England, such hooting was thought to mean hailstorms were coming. To prove such folklore stays with us, ask anyone what the owl stands for and they are likely to say: witches, ghosts, hauntings, and wisdom.

W. J. Brodesip in his book, *Zoological Recreations*, published in London in 1849, summed up the features of the owl that give us every reason to think this is an extraordinary creature: 'Their retired habits, the desolate places that are their favourite haunts, their hollow hootings, fearful shrieks, serpent-like hissings and coffin maker-like snappings, have helped to give them a bad eminence.'

Today, the owl's reputation has been largely restored. He is found in classic children's books like *Winnie the Pooh*. Shops sell many pottery versions of owls and they are a popular motif on greeting cards. Still, that lonely hooting in the garden at midnight makes most people glad to be inside.

The little owl in this design is definitely a friendly one. He lives in a ruined cottage at the beginning of my lane. In the late afternoon he sits on the top of the crumbling chimney stack, no doubt planning his night-time strategy.

Owls in the fir wood mirrored by a
moon / so lucidly bright, you
could find a pin / or thread a
needle by it. I could hear / a fox, a
moth beating its spinnaker /
against the glass, its dusting
mushroom silks. / And nearer,
something ticking, a spider / fiddling in its
web, or the upright fur / of a fieldmouse caught
in an owl's red stare.

'Vibrations', Jeremy Reed, 1985

COLOURWAYS FOR LITTLE OWL
OWL   Browns: A475, A761, A763, A764, A767 (PA401, PA406, PA405, PA403, PA410)   Grey: A962 (PA212)   Black: A993 (PA220)   White: A992 (PA261)
LEAVES   Greens: A242, A245, A404, A407 (PA650, PA602, PA652, PA653)
BORDER   Greens: A242, A404, A407 (PA650, PA652, PA653)
COLOURWAYS FOR BROWN MOTIF
Browns: A301, A303, A305, A311 (PA404, PA483, PA471, PA742)

GRAPES AND LEAVES

Six thousand years ago the Egyptians adorned their walls with paintings of vine bowers, and there never seems to have been a time when humanity did not seek the pleasure and solace of the grape. The Romans brought vine-growing to England, and in the Dark Ages the monks kept alive the skill. By the eighteenth century, wine-making in England had ceased, and in the late 1960s only about ten acres were grown. Today, all that has changed, and there are some thousand acres given over to producing wine.

As a religious symbol, the vine was widely used in church embroideries and linen whitework. The curling tendrils, the delectable shape of the fruit and the masses of leaves appealed to the artist in every embroiderer. The vine remained in domestic needlework, therefore, long after enthusiasm for church decoration faded. Like the strawberry, we instantly rec-ognize those clusters of red, white, green or purple fruit.

It was while sitting in a friend's garden that the idea for the large design formed. The grapes hung almost separate from the leaves on the cottage wall. A bird, nesting between the foliage and the cottage, darted in and out. This little scene of grapes and bird is an old favourite in the decorative arts. It can be found in many examples of eighteenth- and nineteenth-century domestic needlework, such as appliquéd covers, and was also an admired motif for stencilling walls and furniture. The black stitches give this design that folk-art style and simplicity. While ideal for a cushion, the design makes an excellent overall pattern for a small rug. In it there might be only a pair of birds, each to be discovered in a different place as you study the finished work. The red grape repeat pattern is another example of a long-time favourite. This repeating motif of grapes, leaves and tendrils, arranged in precise geometric style, always manages to turn out well. The Victoria and Albert Museum in London, and one of Britain's best known manufacturers of fabrics and wallpapers, both have their versions of the repeating grape motif, only one is Elizabethan and the other a contemporary design. I have used a single colour in my design as I like the overall effect to emerge first when you see the needlework. After that, the detail takes over and the repeat can be seen.

COLOURWAYS FOR GRAPES AND LEAVES

GRAPES AND LEAVES Green: A429 (PA620) Black: A993 (PA220)

BIRD Brown: A904 (PA412) Black: A993 (PA220)

COLOURWAYS FOR RED GRAPES

Red: A503 (PA940)

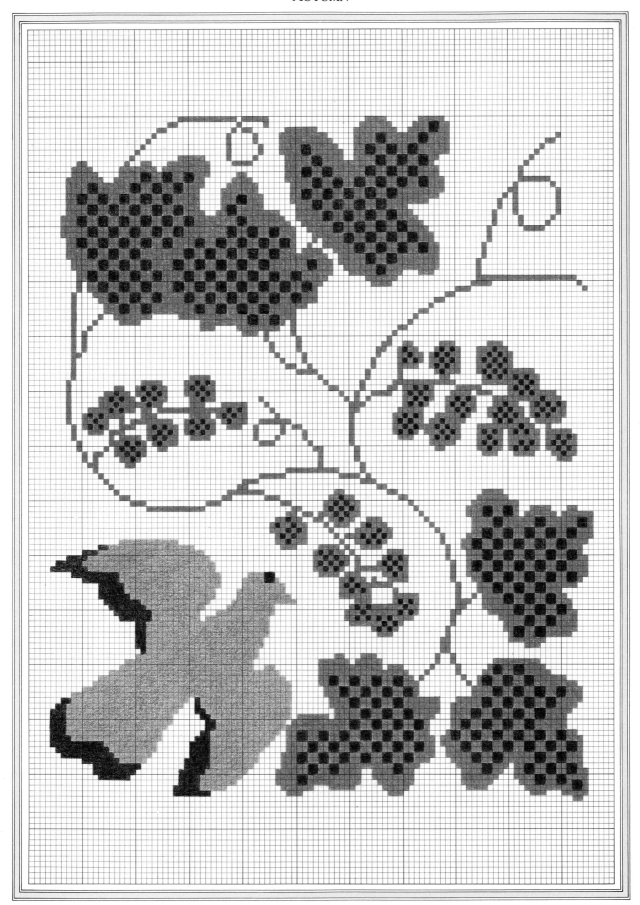

CHINESE LANTERNS

Red rose-hips, the orange bells of Chinese lanterns and the open pods of *Iris foetidissima*, bursting with glossy, red fruit, are the arrangement for this large design. While I am attracted by the exotic quality of this iris, I am never really certain that it belongs in an English garden; it looks as if it should be in a jungle. The leaves give off a rank smell when bruised, which accounts for its common name of 'stinking iris'. The foliage is evergreen, which is helpful, but the plant's sole beauty lies in its seed pods which burst open in autumn. If you pick and dry the seed pods they last quite well in the house.

The way to preserve Chinese lanterns is to cut them when the lanterns or calyces begin to show colour. Decide yourself at which stage you like the colour – whether green turning to orange or with all the lanterns a deep orange. Hang the stems upsidedown to dry. When they have dried, strip off the leaves. The remaining branches with their lanterns fall into a naturally graceful arrangement when put together in a vase. With the addition of rose-hips, the geometric and unstudied quality of autumn foliage is very apparent.

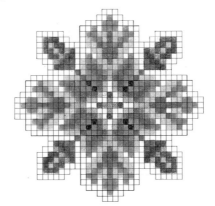

Every oak has been an acorn.

The roundness of berries and rose-hips, and shapes like the lanterns, are not as easily achieved in needlepoint, with its lack of free-flowing curves, as in silk embroidery. But there is little doubt that the bright colours and angular shapes can come across well in tent or cross-stitch. A particular design could, of course, be worked in crewel wool on linen as an alternative to canvas. The results are different but remain variations on a theme.

Oaks have great dignity, growing slowly and living to a great age. They are a precious heritage and there must be few, if any, who would willingly see one cut down. The oak has long been venerated and is involved in many folk legends and traditions. On St John's Day, a piece of oak rubbed on the body is believed to cure open wounds. The oak was the sacred tree of the Celts and Druids and was thought to possess magical powers to help the spirit of prophecy. For this reason, the Druids' altars were located beneath oak trees. The Romans believed certain oaks delivered prophecies, and the ancient Arcadians believed that by stirring water with an oak branch, rain could be commanded to appear.

Royal Oak Day celebrates the restoration of King Charles II and commemorates his concealment in an oak. An ancient oak in the New Forest, the Cadenham Oak, is regarded as sacred because it bursts into bud on Christmas Day. There are other ancient oaks in England called 'Gospel Trees'. These date back to the annual perambulations by villagers of their parish boundaries on Ascension Day, when a portion of the Gospel was read under trees which grew on the boundary lines. Many of these same trees probably had pagan Druidical connections.

COLOURWAYS FOR CHINESE LANTERNS

LANTERNS   Yellows: A551, A553, A555 (PA763, PA773, PA702)   Reds: A441, A862, A864 (PA813, PA815, PA811)   Greens: A251A, A543, A546 (PA672, PA670, PA611)

LEAVES OF LANTERNS   Greens: A251A, A543, A546 (PA672, PA670, PA611)   HIPS   Reds: A862, A994, A995 (PA845, PA842, PA840)

STEMS   Brown: A905 (PA640)

IRIS AND IRIS LEAVES   Greens: A343, A345, A348 (PA653, PA652, PA640)   Reds: A994, A995 (PA844, PA840)   BORDER   Reds: A862, A994, A995 (PA845, PA843, PA840)

COLOURWAYS FOR OAK LEAVES AND ACORNS

LEAVES   Greens: A253, A403, A406, A407 (PA678, PA621, PA611, PA660)   Browns: A624, A722 (PA403, PA401)   Yellow: A872 (PA724)

ACORNS   Browns: A903, A915 (PA751, PA401)   Yellow: A842 (PA700)   Greens: A406, A545, A547 (PA660, PA642, PA644)

FALLEN LEAVES

Here are some leaves as they blew into my garden – brown, red, orange, yellow, gold, silver, black, green and dying dark. Go out and gather some of your own. Put them on a table near you and look at the colours and have a go at some freehand embroidery. A stitch here and a stitch there, a few for the stems, and another leaf behind. If you don't want to start with this idea, then do some from my design, but try to add a few of your own. The nice thing about using leaves in embroidery is that everyone can create a leaf in needlepoint that looks like a leaf to everyone else. Such categorical statements are rarely safe to make but this is one – your leaf may not look like an oak, maple, ash, poplar or birch leaf, but it will look like *some kind* of leaf. The arrangement of leaves in this design is absolutely random, just as they are found fallen in nature. It doesn't matter which side of the leaf you use; there is no right or wrong side, shape or position for autumn leaves. This little reality caused me to let the leaf at the bottom of my design fall over the border frame.

O Wild West Wind, thou breath of Autumn's
*   being,*
Thou from whose unseen presence the leaves
*   dead*
Are driven like ghosts from an enchanter
*   fleeing,*

'Ode to the West Wind',
Percy Bysshe Shelley, 1792-1822

The border itself is based on a wooden Victorian picture frame and it is useful for many designs in the book. Alter the four colours of the border to match or blend with whatever central pattern you are producing. The border for Fallen Leaves helps to hold them as a picture.

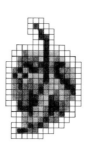

I let the leaves lie where they fall in my garden. By the time the trees are bare, I am indoors anyway, planning Christmas and resigned to the advent of winter. The leaves protect whatever lies beneath from frost, and some rot away to enrich the soil. If they are still about in the spring, then I may clear them away. Whether this is good gardening practice or not, I don't know. It is what happens in nature and wild strawberries are delicious and wild violets pretty, so why shouldn't the plants in my garden enjoy the same protection of the leaves? So be it.

How long will the hand of the woods in
the rain come close to me with all its needles
to weave the high kisses of the foliage
*   Again*
I listen to the approach, like that of
a fire in smoke, of the birth of the light
full of petals from the ash of earth,
*   and dividing the ground*
into a river of white ears the sun reaches
my mouth like an old buried tear that
has become seed again.

'Naciendo en los Bosques', Pablo Neruda,
Selected Poems, 1970

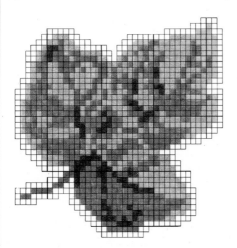

COLOURWAYS FOR FALLEN LEAVES
Greens: A256, A542, A545 (PA690, PA670, PA692)   Yellow: A844 (PA702)   Brown: A915 (PA421)   Reds: A206, A208, A503, A505, A694, A696, A944 (PA403, PA401, PA951, PA940, PA724, PA722, PA955)   Black: A998 (PA221)
BORDER   A694, A844, A696, A915, A208 (PA724, PA702, PA722, PA421, PA401)

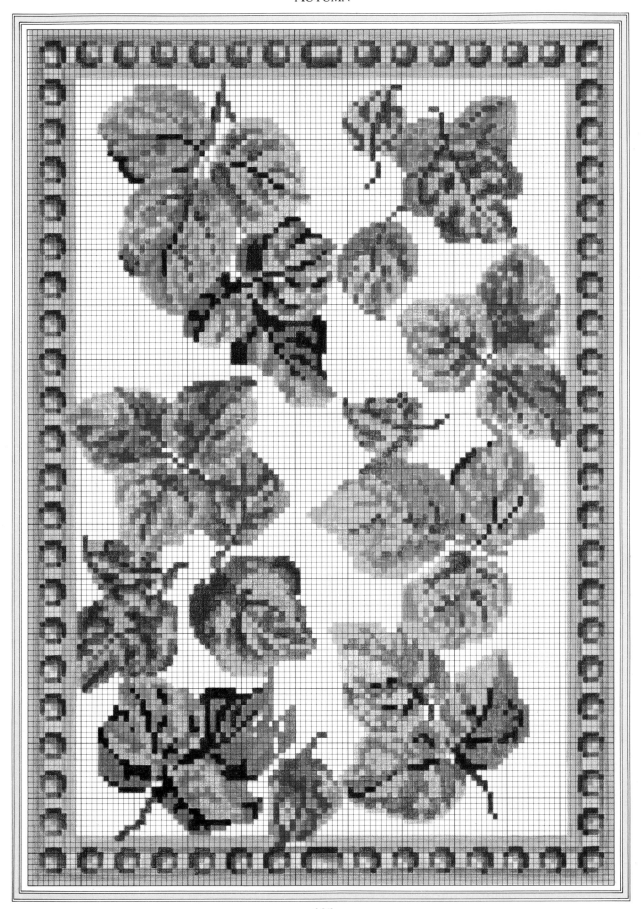

BUCKFAST CYCLAMENS

I made the sketches for this design of cyclamens along the garden walk of Buckfast Abbey, a Benedictine monastery which nestles by the River Dart in Devon. The walkway starts at the Abbey and goes along the river, which was overhung with gold and red trees the autumn I was there. Sitting on a bench enjoying the quiet, I spotted rose-pink cyclamens which had been planted at random under some trees.

There are many species of hardy cyclamen which grow only a few inches tall and it is possible to have different sorts blooming from August almost through to the spring. I think that the Abbey ones were *Cyclamen neapolitanum album* which have rose-pink flowers and dark green marbled leaves. Cyclamen flowers stand proudly above the plant's heart-shaped leaves which are often variegated. In my design I have given three patterns: the central panel of flowers and leaves; the surrounding trellis-work; and the border. Each may be used successfully for separate embroideries.

You might like, for example, to put another plant in the centre panel and then, changing the colours to those of the new flowers, use the same surround and border. The central panel without the cyclamens would be ideal for a name, initials or a short saying.

Over half a million people come to visit the Abbey, to walk through its grounds, and to admire the work of these monks whose history here has been so remarkable. The monastery, founded in 1018, experienced centuries of peace, ruin when Henry VIII dissolved the monasteries in England in 1539, and, finally, restoration in 1907 when the monks returned to rebuild their abbey. The great Abbey church was finished in 1937, largely restored to its original form. When you see this soaring building and admire its fine stonework, marble mosaics and other works of art, it is hard to believe that a team of only six monks could have built the place – but it is so. Here, much to many people's surprise, is a *modern* work to the glory of God.

Almost opposite the patch of cyclamens I sketched, stands the home village of the Abbey's famous bees. Enclosed within a low wall, you enter the village through a wrought-iron gate. The old-fashioned hives are like small cottages, each painted pink with a rose-coloured roof and a number plate over the front door, and arranged in orderly 'streets'. The impression of a village is heightened by the fact that the hives are placed on each side of a path down the middle. This path leads to the bee-keeper's office, which is also painted pink and rose. It is a magical sight to come upon as you walk through the Abbey grounds and the bees that live there are no ordinary ones for the Buckfast Bee is justly famous.

This is how it happened. Before the First World War, England was swept by a disease which wiped out all its bees. A monk, Brother Adam, set out to breed a new kind of bee that would resist such diseases. He succeeded, and today Buckfast Bee stock is exported around the world from Texas to Israel. Brother Adam's discoveries, techniques and books about bees are internationally recognized. The monastery keeps some 320 hives and produces masses of delicious heather and clover honey.

Stands the Church clock at ten to three?
And is there honey still for tea?
'The Old Vicarage, Grantchester',
Rupert Brooke, 1887-1915

Although Buckfast is famous for many things from bees, honey and a herbal tonic wine to the creation of stained-glass windows and teaching, its primary purpose is prayer, and the real work of all the monks is to seek communion with God. Such contemplation is not something easy to understand or even to describe. St John of the Cross found the allegory of love – and flowers – helped him a little to explain: 'I abandoned and forgot myself / Laying my face on my Belovèd; / All things ceased; I went out from myself / Leaving my cares / Forgotten among the lilies.'

COLOURWAYS FOR BUCKFAST CYCLAMENS

FLOWERS   Purples: A455, A801 (PA311, PA353)
Red: A942 (PA945)   LEAVES   Greens: A543, A832
(PA634, PA620)   White: A991 (PA262)
TRELLIS   Green: A832 (PA620)   Red: A801 (PA353)
BORDER   Purples: A455, A801 (PA311,
PA353)   Red: A942 (PA945)   Greens: A543,
A832 (PA634, PA620)   White: A991 (PA262)

And glow more intense than blaze of branch, or
    brazier,
Stirs the dumb spirit: no wind, but pentecostal fire
In the dark time of the year. Between melting and
    freezing
The soul's sap quivers. There is no earth smell
Or smell of living thing. This is the spring time
But not in time's covenant. Now the hedgerow
Is blanched for an hour with transitory blossom
Of snow, a bloom more sudden
Than that of summer, neither budding nor fading,
Not in the scheme of generation.
Where is the summer? the unimaginable
Zero summer?
 'Little Gidding', Thomas Stearns Eliot, 1888-1965

WINTER

After the autumn displays, the garden in winter seems difficult to admire, but it is only that the colours, tones and shapes have changed so dramatically that we need time to get used to more subtle discoveries. In designs for embroidery, we need to move away from the dominance of colour and find instead structure and contrast. When winter colours do appear, they are notable because they stand out so much.

There is plenty to track down and discover in the winter garden: flowers like asters are still there; holly berries; the fruits of Chinese lanterns; viburnum; the autumn cherry *Prunus subhirtella*, which blooms from November to almost the end of March; and winter-flowering jasmine. If you are lucky and have only slight frosts, then there may be camellias. The bell-like flowers of *Clematis balearica* come and go all the season, and Chinese witch-hazel is a first-rate star of the winter show. The yellow and gold display of stiff, formal *Mahonia japonica* and the Christmas rose, *Helleborus niger*, complete a short winter garden walk. Coloured barks, tree shapes, and the foliage of all the evergreens are in the background, so winter is hardly barren. It is a time to appreciate things one by one, a time to heighten our ability to observe and appreciate, to define and refine all we see, and, hopefully, to capture a few of them in embroidery.

Red sky at night, Shepherd's delight,
Red in the morning, Shepherd's warning.
Old Saying

Winter is the season of most complaints about the weather. Will it never stop raining or snowing or hailing or blowing? Can we dare that wind? Should I take an umbrella just in case? Even if the summer was hot, the winter will please few people no matter what happens. It is a rare voice that can be heard proclaiming satisfaction. One such voice was that of the inimitable Jane Austen. She wrote to her sister in December 1815 full of praise: 'I enjoy it all over me, from top to toe, from right to left, longitudinally, perpendicularly, diagonally; and I cannot but selfishly hope we are to have it last till Christmas – nice, unwholesome, unseasonable, relaxing, close, muggy weather.' Not for Miss Austen the crisp, bracing cold that sends the rest of us scurrying gratefully home to the fire.

If there were dreams to sell,
Merry and sad to tell,
And the crier rang the bell,
What would you buy?
'Dream-Pedlary', Thomas Lovell Beddoes,
1798-1851

Mistletoe, forgotten for the rest of the year, is hunted down now for the Christmas holiday. This plant with its white pearls, sharply defined leaves and destructive habit, seems to play no other role in our lives except to provide an excuse for kissing. This custom, reinforced ages ago by the Druids, who thought the plant magical, comes from an ancient legend which says that mistletoe was given into the keeping of the goddess of love. It was ordained by her that any one passing beneath it should receive a kiss to show love not hate. Once, when I was coming out of the London Underground, a middle-aged

A sprig of holly from *The Flowers of Shakespeare*, circa 1845.

ticket collector held a twig of mistletoe over the heads of every male passenger she fancied, claiming both a ticket and a kiss. Young or old, no man refused her. The strength of legend or the nature of man?

I knew a girl who was so pure
She couldn't say the word Manure.
Indeed, her modesty was such,
She wouldn't pass a rabbit hutch;
And butterflies upon the wing
Would make her blush like anything.

That lady is a gardener now,
And all her views have changed, somehow.
She squashes greenfly with her thumb,
And knows how little snowdrops come:
In fact, the garden she has got,
Has broadened out her mind a lot.
'A Perfect Lady', Reginald Arkell, 1882-1959

The colours of the winter garden for the embroiderer are never dull. They can often be vivid and more striking than those of autumn. It is the unexpected contrast that makes it so. For example, in my design for January leaves the reds are more intense than those of autumn because the contrast between the green and red of the leaves is greater. The blues and whites of cold air and clear night are there in the designs of snowflakes. Above all, the berries offer inspiration – red, orange, purple, yellow, black, blue, burgundy – the assortment is like a handful of beautiful marbles. Robins, holly, ivy and Christmas bring cheer too, and, hopefully, plans for new needlework.

It is at Christmas and the other great celebrations of the church calendar that we see some magnificent treasures of ecclesiastical embroidery, including floral art at its pinnacle of success. Church embroidery provided a fruitful environment for the development of needlework as an art from the earliest times until about the eighteenth century. The widespread popularity of the craft among amateurs then made it an imitative pastime much given to the copying of other works of art and dominated by rules of technique.

In the church, lavishly embroidered copes were greatly admired and, indeed, these are still to be seen today in many Roman, Anglo-Catholic and Greek churches. In the thirteenth and fourteenth centuries English church embroidery earned such a high reputation that it was known as *opus anglicanum*. It was much favoured by the popes of the time, and there are some fine examples in the papal treasury. Works of this period are divided into three parts. From about 1250 to 1275 embroidery depicted saints and scenes from the bible, enclosed within medallions. The second stage, ranging from 1275 to 1325, brought greater freedom of design. From about 1325 to the end of that century, animals, birds, flowers, foliage and angels were among the many things portrayed on vestments. This is considered by many art historians to be the golden age of English ecclesiastical embroidery. After the Reformation, much of the embroidery was removed from the church and used for secular and domestic purposes. Lord Darnley, for example, consort of Mary Queen of Scots, had a bed covering and curtaining made from a cope, chasuble and four tunicles in about 1562.

There has been an exciting revival of church embroidery in Britain since the Second World War. The first work was modernistic but in the last few years there has been much interest in many Anglican churches in elaborate vestments with gold work and fine beading.

While making church kneelers has become popular among amateur needleworkers, many significant new church embroideries have been commissioned. Some examples one can easily see are those of the cushions and wall panels for the fourteenth-century stalls in Wells Cathedral, and the remarkable work of Beryl Dean MBE – for example, the vestments she made for the Bishop of London on the occasion of the Queen's Silver Jubilee in 1977. Other outstanding original work is being done by the nuns at the Priory of Our Lady of Peace, Turvey Abbey in Bedfordshire.

Modern ecclesiastical embroidery has not escaped the movement toward abstraction in embroidery design, and the more earnest than successful attempts during the 1960s and 1970s to free embroidery as an art form from the restrictions and limitations of traditional techniques and rules. Recent works, however, have seen a return to iconoclastic and representational design to which most people can easily relate and which recognizably reflects Christian biblical stories and symbolism.

It is always good when a man has two irons in the fire.
'The Faithful Friends', John Fletcher, 1579-1625

There is hardly an embroiderer who cannot shake out a drawer of wools and unfinished work – often intended as Christmas gifts. The embroiderer's habit which most seems to trouble those who don't do needlework is the number of these unfinished pieces! 'You aren't going to buy *more* wool are you?', they ask. 'But you have plenty of *those* at home you haven't used yet!', they cry as we buy some new canvas or wool.

However, having more than one thing 'on the go' is a trait all needleworkers seem to share. My own cupboard is filled high with such things: some fine silks, all lavenders, washed greens and sea shell pinks, bought on a trip to Germany; a giant canvas handed to me in France by a famous weaver of small napkins and fine linen with the command that I should make a needle-

point rug; some seventeenth-century embroidery rescued one afternoon in a Liverpool shop and still holding within it the fragile scent of age; a selection of wools once organized by shades but now a mixed bouquet; a Victorian stool cover to be repaired for a friend who has been waiting without complaint for three years. My cupboard is full of work to be done, of bits and pieces to inspire and remind, and of years to come of enjoyment. It is as it should be – a cupboard of good intentions.

Winter, then, is a time to sit down in front of the fire and let your memory wander while your hands are pleasantly occupied with stitching. We can give to ourselves that seasonal and kindly message: 'Peace be with you.'

BLUE ROSE HIPS

As the world darkens into January and the skies ready for snow, rose hips shine out. At first only spots of red and orange in the garden, they deepen into purple and mahogany. As the hips dry and shrink, the remaining leaves nearby become dark red, then black, and fall away until only the hips are left. These cling through most of the winter and seem to vanish overnight when the frost finally refuses, even at noon, to go away.

And glory, like the phoenix 'midst her fires,
Exhales her odours, blazes, and expires.
Lord Byron, 1788-1824

When I see this final display, the romantic names of the old varieties – Reine des Violettes, Belle d'Amour – help me to recall their summer glory. But the hips are as decorative in their way as the blooms. The shapes can vary greatly. Some are fat globes of orange, while others are long slim flasks that cover the bush in great red sprays. Such hips can be found in many embroidered bands and motifs of the sixteenth and seventeenth centuries.

Arranged as they are on bare branches, the hips show up well in a winter bouquet of berries, ivy leaves and witch-hazel.

In spite of the attractive colours of rose hips, I decided to do some in blue. The practice in needlework of changing the colours of what we normally see in flowers, fruits and leaves has a long tradition. It can turn the ordinary into something special.

At Canon's Ashby House, Northamptonshire, the home of the poet Dryden's family since the sixteenth century, there is a magnificent set of needleworked chairs, settee and fire-screen. While originally probably done in various colours, these pieces today have turned to red and blue through age and the effects of sunlight. The result is striking, while retaining the recognizable shapes of the plants. I have tried to achieve this effect deliberately in the large design of blue rose hips.

The border uses the same range of colours as the central design, but the pattern is abstracted shapes of hips and leaves. For the background of the large design, I would use a pale yellow or

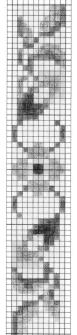

continue the border green throughout. Using the same colour will lose much of the framing effect of this border, resulting in a dense-looking pattern. You may find this pleasing.

Don't overlook the fruit of the common dog or brier rose found in hedgerows and tangled in the boundaries of many country gardens. These small hips, organized with a military precision in clusters along their branches, are the delight of birds and mice. They are the hips most often found portrayed in early embroideries.

The hip ripens when the calyx leaves around the top fall, leaving the fruit soft and fleshy. They appear first in October but last well into January in the area where I live. Once they were gathered and eaten as a dessert, and the English herbalist Gerard says: 'the fruit when it is ripe maketh the most pleasante meats and banketting dishes as tartes and such-like.'

During the Second World War, gathering rose hips in England returned to fashion when food high in vitamin C was needed. The hips were made into jelly or a syrup. Rose hip syrup is still sold in Britain for infants and children, but medical opinion has turned against it because of the high amount of sugar used in the preparation.

Rose hip tea, however, remains a favourite. You can buy it in teabags, often mixed with dried apple and lemon and orange peel – or make your own. To one cup of dried rose hips add a quarter of a cup of dried lemon balm leaves, a teaspoon of dried and grated lemon rind and a stick of cinnamon. Sweeten to taste with honey.

COLOURWAYS FOR BLUE ROSE HIPS
Blues: A741, A744, A746, A749, A876 (PA213, PA500, PA502, PA504, PA506)   Yellow: A471 (PA762)   Reds: A861, A994, A995 (PA840, PA855, PA861)   Black: A998 (PA221)   Purples: A931, A933, A934 (PA321, PA322, PA326)
BORDER   Blues: A741, A746 (PA545, PA560)   Yellow: A471 (PA762)   Red: A995 (PA840)   Black: A998 (PA221)   Purples: A931, A934 (PA922, PA920)
BORDER BACKGROUND   Green: A421 (PA623)

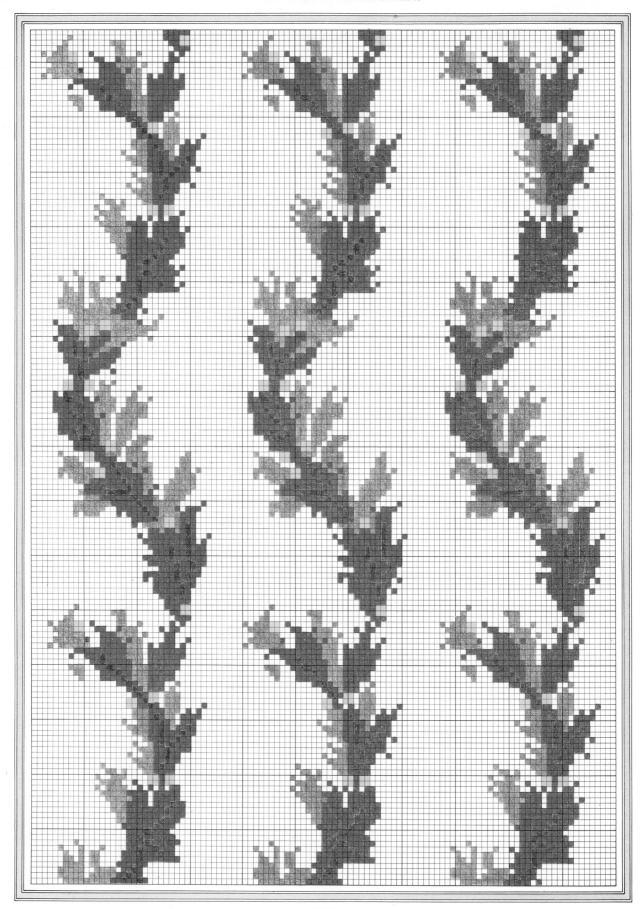

YELLOW BERRY HOLLY

Country lore has it that the birds in winter save the holly berries until last as an emergency ration. In a hard year, the tale seems true, but then in a mild spell the berries are gone in a flash. Is it appetite or just greed? In any case, while they last, the holly sports berries and leaves that brighten any garden.

One of the prettiest hollies is *Ilex aquifolium* 'Bacciflava', a form of common English holly. It has dense dark leaves and bright yellow berries. In the large design, I have drawn branches in a row so that, repeated, they produce a geometric effect.

Red or orange could be substituted for the yellow berries, as the shape of holly leaves is more or less constant from variety to variety. For the background I chose a pale fawn wool.

Out in the dark over the snow
The fallow fawns invisible go
With the fallow doe;
And the winds blow
Fast as the stars are slow.

Stealthily the dark haunts round
And, when the lamp goes, without sound
At a swifter bound
Than the swiftest hound,
Arrives, and all else is drowned;

And star and I and wind and deer,
Are in the dark together, – near,
Yet far, – and fear
Drums on my ear
In that sage company drear.

How weak and little is the light,
All the universe of sight,
Love and delight,
Before the might,
If you love it not, of night.
    'Out in the Dark', Edward Thomas, 1878-1917

There are several other hollies in the garden, such as 'Silver Queen' and 'Golden Queen' which have, respectively, silver- and gold-margined

Leaf and Berry

leaves. In the Yellow Berry Holly design you could change to these other varieties by using white or gold wool to outline each leaf. If you try this, substitute the final outer stitch in each dark green leaf with one of white or gold. Do the same for the central vein of the leaf, which is shown as brown in my design. Change the berries to red, orange or pink.

The other plant that belongs to the English winter is ivy. So often considered an enemy by gardeners, who fear it will strangle trees and shrubs, it offers flowers when all else in the garden is asleep, bearing fruit and hosting birds and late bees and moths. On old walls already weakened by aged mortar and in trees like birch, where an abundance of light makes ivy grow too well, the plant may need cutting and control – but a garden or wood would be poorer for lack of this green winter veil.

Oh roses for the flush of youth,
    And laurel for the perfect prime;
But pluck an ivy branch for me,
    Grown old before my time.
                    'Oh, Roses for the Flush'
                    Christina Rossetti, 1830-1894

Small motif designs, such as the one here for Leaf and Berry, can be repeated over a canvas to form a very different effect. They may be scattered or ordered into lines. I did a small cushion using four of the motifs, one in each quarter of the canvas. Around each, I put a line the same colour red as the berries and used a neutral cream grounding.

COLOURWAYS FOR YELLOW BERRY HOLLY
Greens: A354, A406 (PA613, PA611)   Yellow: A474 (PA712)   Red: A725 (PA920)
COLOURWAYS FOR LEAF AND BERRIES
Greens: A337, A341, A345, A347 (PA690, PA644, PA643, PA640)   Yellow: A693 (PA752)   Brown: A905 (PA430)   Reds: A505, A994, A995 (PA840, PA845, PA843)

SNOWFLAKES

Romantic as snow can be, it may well defeat most embroiderers, for white on white makes a stylish interior but an ineffective canvaswork. Cream on white strains the eyes, and standing back from the finished work, it is hard to distinguish the design. No doubt there are many needleworkers – in addition to those still labouring away at traditional whitework – who have achieved amazing results with white on white and, indeed, with snow effects. I am not one of them.

However, crystals, or what we call snowflakes are a different matter. Each is a complex, fantastic design, none exactly like the other. As you might suspect, snowflakes are familiar objects in Scandinavian embroidery, particularly cross-stitch. While snow occurs most frequently about freezing point, when the temperature falls below this, as it regularly does in the far North, the snow becomes individual crystals with a great variety of forms – needles, plates, prisms and stars.

These forms are easy to create in embroidery. In fact, stylized flowers often end up looking like snowflakes. If they are stitched in blues, as I have done, it helps to underline that they *are* snowflakes. It is important to remember that every crystal is perfectly symmetrical. It is this feature which allows them to be dissembled and the various parts used to form another motif. For example, the small flakes on this page are taken from the ones in the large design. You may discover others.

If you insist on bringing snow as blankets of white into your embroidery of the garden in winter, then I suggest you study Chinese and Japanese paintings. They seem able to show snow on plants and branches with a lightness of definition that might translate into silk on fine mesh canvas.

It was probably the Chinese too who originally used snow and ice to cool drinks and create ices and frozen creams.

Perhaps winter is not the usual time to think of summer treats, but one thing leads to another, so here is a recipe for smoked tea ice-cream. It confers on a cup of hot tea an entirely new role in your life!

SMOKED TEA ICE-CREAM
For this dish, a variation on one by Nathalie Hambro in her book *Particular Delights*, you will need the following: *1 pint (500 ml) milk (use fresh goat's milk if you can get it); 3 tablespoons Lapsang Souchong tea; 1 tablespoon rosewater; 6 large egg yolks; 6 oz (175g) vanilla-flavoured caster sugar; 2 egg whites; 1 tablespoon of water.* Heat the milk without boiling it. Add the tea leaves and simmer for 15 minutes. Stir in the rosewater. In another pan beat the egg yolks and 4 oz (125g) of the sugar until the mixture is frothy. Add the strained milk a little at a time. Put this to simmer slowly in a *bain marie* until it has a custard consistency – do not let it boil. When ready, set this mixture aside to cool. Next

beat the egg whites until stiff. Put the remaining sugar in the water and stir until dissolved. Boil this for about two minutes and then pour it straight on to the whites, beating until the whole thing is cool. Chill. Finally, blend the two mixtures and freeze for a minimum of three hours. Remove from the freezer and put into the refrigerator about 45 minutes before serving.

COLOURWAYS FOR SNOWFLAKES
Blues: A464, A481 (PA501, PA594)
BORDER Blues: A464, A821
(PA502, PA563)

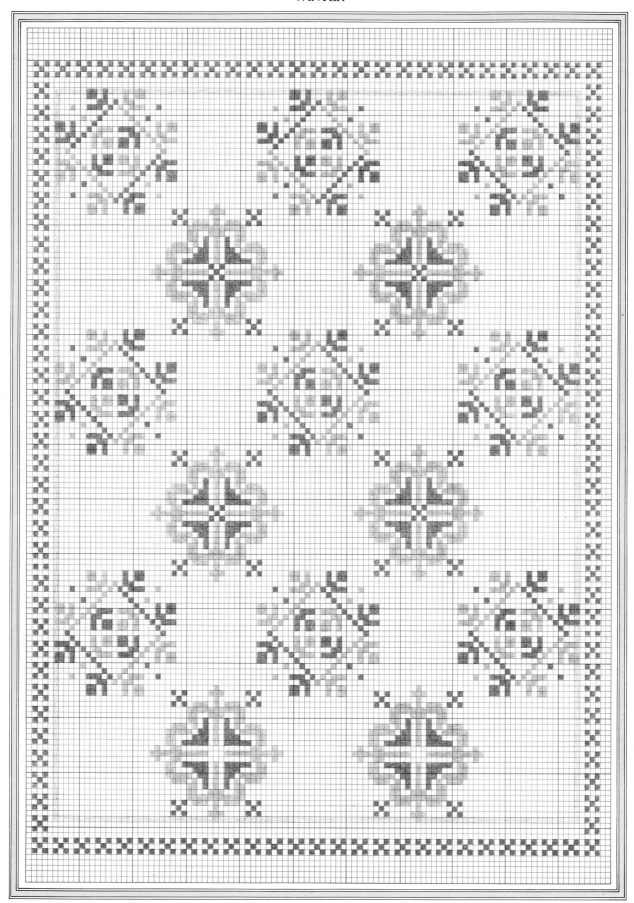

JANUARY LEAVES

The earth covering the flower beds is a brown blanket under which sleep many promises – crocuses, daffodils, narcissi, the perennial plants with summer flowers to come, the snow-drops stirring into first life, and all the weeds to keep you busy. Out there in the dark are seed and root and secret.

As the generation of leaves, so is that of men.
The Illiad, Homer, c.900 BC

Rolling around and blowing up into corners, against fences and across paths, are wet fallen leaves. From a distance they give a forlorn look to the garden. On closer inspection they offer both colour and pattern to the embroiderer. There are patchworks of brown and silver, red and orange, copper and grey, yellow and gold.

But there are more than leaves about in January. You may spot very early narcissus *Daphne mezereum* in her pink flowers, the yellow stars of witch-hazel, some *Iris unguicularis*, a few crocuses, and struggling through old grass and weeds, some perky blue buds of pulmonaria. For me the true beauty of January remains the bare trees, wet leaves, wild skies and long damp walks while planning for spring. True, I keep looking at the honeysuckle on the fence to see if life is stirring, but then honeysuckle is like an all-night shop – it hardly ever closes for business.

Then the moon came quiet and flooded full
Light and beauty on clouds like wool,
On a feasted fox at rest from hunting,
In the beech-wood grey where the brocks were
grunting.
The beech-wood grey rose dim in the night
With moonlight fallen in pools of light,
The long dead leaves on the ground were rimed;
A clock struck twelve and the church-bells
chimed.

John Masefield, 1878-1967

The large design of leaves is from a bush by the rear walk at the manor house in my village. The dark leaves with bright red centres and margins are dramatic and unexpected. No-one seems to know the name of the bush and I decided to leave it as a mystery appropriate to the dark day and the old house.

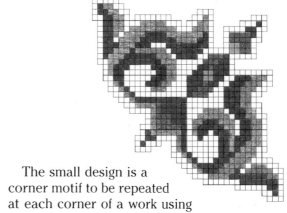

The small design is a corner motif to be repeated at each corner of a work using the same colours as for the leaves. It has no particular relationship to January or winter, but could be used wherever some kind of framing is necessary to help hold a central pattern together. Change the motif colours to suit your own scheme. Another interesting way to use the motif would be to place four together in the centre of a canvas to form a single elaborate design.

COLOURWAYS FOR JANUARY LEAVES
Greens: A402, A404, A407 (PA614, PA612, PA610)   Reds: A501A, A502, A505, A861 (PA853, PA851, PA840, PA855)
COLOURWAYS FOR CORNER MOTIFS
Greens: A403, A404 (PA614, PA612)   Reds: A502, A505 (PA858, PA851)   Black: A998 (PA221)

A corner motif which can be used in any colours.

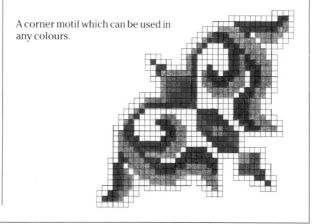

A CHRISTMAS ROBIN

The robin with its cheerful red breast and fierce individualism has long been a favourite with English embroiderers. The little bird follows the gardener if digging is to be done, sitting close by to spot newly unearthed worms. In this design I have shown a robin puffed-up against the cold and sitting on that other favourite of winter and Christmas time – the holly.

The holly and the ivy,
When they are both full grown,
Of all the trees that are in the wood,
The holly bears the crown:
The rising of the sun
And the running of the deer,
The playing of the merry organ,
Sweet singing in the choir.
  'The Holly and the Ivy', Oxford Book of Carols

All these things seem to belong to one another. Flora Thompson, writing of the seasons of the English year, said, 'December and January are the bare months. Our grandmothers, when they compiled their floral calendar, could not find a flower for December at all and took the holly-berry instead. Their choice is understandable. Christmas and holly, holly and Christmas. Who could think of one without the other?'

Pies of mincemeat,
An ear asleep,
A smell of cooking,
A merry feast,
A meaty turkey,
A roasting aroma,
Apron oligarchy.
A post quota,
A priest at prayer
A tasselled altar.
  'Christmas', Christopher Nolan

The bird-on-branch motif is common to the embroidery of many European countries. The kind of bird varies according to the area. During the height of Berlin work in Victorian times, the parrot was a great favourite as a caged bird, and this is reflected in the number of examples remaining of Berlin work parrots. Today, these look particularly of their period with their stump of padded flowers and often beaded leaves surrounding the bird. They are usually large works, and with the wool colours then used, coupled with the briliant plumage of most parrots, the pieces are not easy to fit into a modern setting.

There is one more ingredient for a happy Christmas – children. In spite of amazing toys and electronic gadgetry, an older child might still be pleased to have this robin and his holly as a cushion. You could put the child's name under the framed robin and add this little poem, a line above each of the four sides of the frame.

Little Robin Redbreast
Came to visit me;
This is what he whistled,
Thank you for my tea.
  Old English Rhyme

December, then, draws the year to a close and marks midwinter as the garden falls into sleep. Although we may grumble about the wet and cold, daydream over seed catalogues, and make many plans that will bear no fruit save to pass an hour, nature is at work, and it is the best time of year to take up the needle, select some wools and start work on a new embroidery. The work of nature will always be more perfect than our own and, in a way, the centuries of embroidered flowers and animals are in praise of her delights and our gardens. I think this sampler inscription about needlework done by an English girl in 1831 serves well as a motto for any work which we may do:

In the glad morn of blooming youth
These various threads I drew,
And now behold this finished piece
Lies glorious to the view.
So when bright youth shall charm no more
And age shall chill my blood,
May I review my life and say,
Behold my works are good.

COLOURWAYS FOR CHRISTMAS ROBIN

BIRD Greys: A962, A963, A964 (PA204, PA202, PA200) Brown: A587 (PA450) Reds: A502, A995 (PA842, PA931) Black: A993 (PA220) Yellows: A695, A698 (PA732, PA411)
LEAVES Greens: A423, A694 (PA611, PA612) Black: A993 (PA221)
BERRIES Reds: A501A, A995 (PA970, PA840)

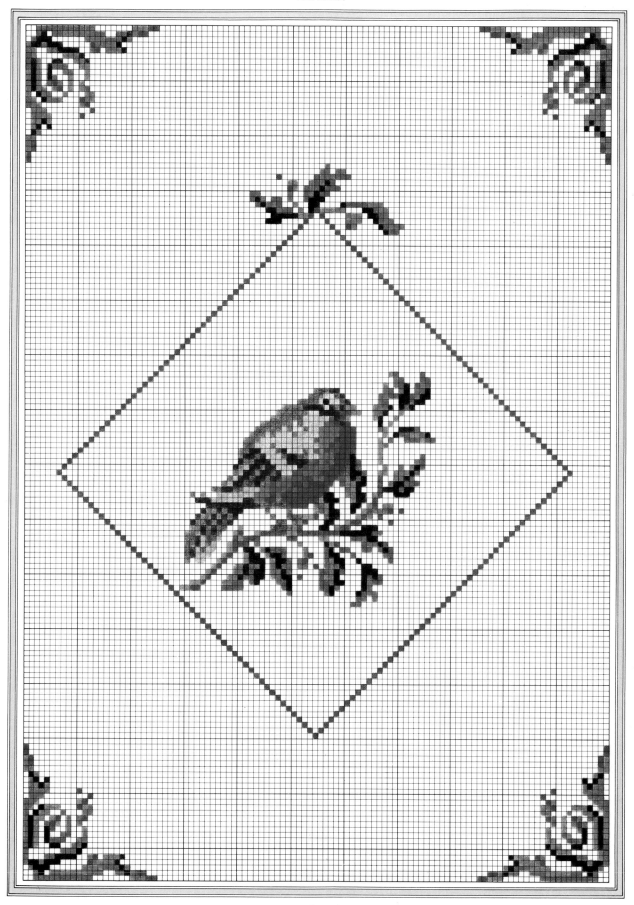

ACKNOWLEDGEMENTS

I am grateful to Stanley Duller and Jo Corfield for their help. I am also grateful to the following individuals and publishers who gave their permission to reproduce the following verse and prose: 'He Wishes for the Cloths of Heaven', William Butler Yeats, from *The Collected Poems of W. B. Yeats*, courtesy of A. P. Watt Ltd, on behalf of Michael B. Yeats and Macmillan, London, and Macmillan, New York; 3 lines by Virgil from *Roman Poetry from the Republic to the Silver Age*, translated by Dorothea Wender, courtesy of Southern Illinois University Press; 4 lines of 'The Glory of the Garden', Rudyard Kipling, from *The Definitive Edition of Rudyard Kipling's Verse*, courtesy of A. P. Watt Ltd, on behalf of the National Trust; *The Butterfly Gardener*, Miriam Rothschild, courtesy of The Rainbird Publishing Group Ltd; 'Vibrations', Jeremy Reed, courtesy of Jeremy Reed; 'Reluctance', Robert Frost, from *The Poetry of Robert Frost* edited by Edward Connery Lathem, courtesy of the Estate of Robert Frost, Jonathan Cape Ltd and Holt, Rinehart and Winston, New York; 10 lines from 'Naciendo en los Bosques', Pablo Neruda, translated by W. S. Merwin from *Selected Poems* edited by Nathaniel Tarn, courtesy of the Estate of Pablo Neruda, Jonathan Cape Ltd and Seymour Lawrence Inc., Boston; 'There Came a Day', Ted Hughes, reprinted from *Season Songs* by Ted Hughes courtesy of Faber and Faber Ltd and Viking Press, New York; 12 lines of 'Little Gidding', T. S. Eliot, reprinted from *Four Quartets* by T. S. Eliot courtesy of Faber and Faber Ltd and Harcourt Brace Jovanovich Inc., Florida; 'Fern Hill', Dylan Thomas, from *Collected Poems* by Dylan Thomas, courtesy of J. M. Dent & Sons Ltd and New Directions Publishing Corporation, New York.

The publishers would like to thank the Bridgeman Art Library for permission to reproduce the following paintings: George Samuel Elgood (1851-1943), *Garden Scene*, pp. 8-9; P. J. Redouté (1759-1840), *Bengale The Hymenée from Les Choix des plus Belles Fleurs*, p. 21; G. D. Ehret (1708-1770), *Hepatica Trifolia*, p. 34.

The publishers would also like to thank the Fine Art Photographic Library Ltd for permission to reproduce the following paintings: William Charles Thomas Dobson (1817-1898), *Christmas Roses*, p. 22; Maude Goodman (fl. 1874-1901), *The Little Flower Child*, p. 13; Theresa Sylvester Stannard (1898-1947), *A Cottage Garden*, p. 25; Charles Edward Wilson (fl. 1891-1936), *A Girl at the Gate*, pp. 26-27; anonymous (19th century), *Primroses*, p. 48; Percy Tarrant (1883-1904), *Picking Roses*, p. 32; Frederick Morgan (1856-1927), *Picking Apples*, p. 6; George Sheridan Knowles (1863-1931), *Feeding the Pigeons*, p. 14; Annie Mary Youngman (1860-1919), *Hellebores*, p. 23; (illustration published 1803) *Grass-leaved Flag*, p. 76; anonymous (c. 1845), Holly from *The Flowers of Shakespeare*, p. 130; Ernest Llewellyn Hampshire, *A Summer Cottage Garden*, pp. 18-19; Eugene-Henri Cauchois (1850-1911), *Still Lives of Flowers: Spring, Summer, Autumn & Winter*, pp. 46, 74, 108 and 128.

Finally, the publishers would like to thank: the Mansell Collection for permission to reproduce *Grapes in a Basket*, p. 30; a Private Collection for permission to reproduce G. D. Ehret (1708-1770), *Jargonelle Pear*, p. 110; the Victoria & Albert Museum for permission to reproduce G. D. Ehret (1708-1770), *Le Perroquet Rouge*, p. 10; the Norfolk Museums Service (Norwich Castle Museum) for permission to reproduce Eloise Harriet Stannard (1829-1915), *Overturned Raspberries, White Currants and Roses*, p. 31; and the author for permission to reproduce *Tulips* by James Hall Hopkins, p. 49, and the original *Berlin Artwork* pattern, p. 28.